I0142786

I AM

"I AM" JEHOVAH, THE KING AND LORD OF ISRAEL - "I AM" JESUS, THE KING AND LORD OF CHRISTIANS

Jim Taylor

NEW HARBOR PRESS

Rapid City, SD

Copyright © 2023 by Jim Taylor.

All rights reserved. No part of this publication may be reproduced, distributed or transmitted in any form or by any means, including photocopying, recording, or other electronic or mechanical methods, without the prior written permission of the publisher, except in the case of brief quotations embodied in critical reviews and certain other noncommercial uses permitted by copyright law. For permission requests, write to the publisher, addressed "Attention: Permissions Coordinator," at the address below.

Taylor/New Harbor Press
1601 Mt Rushmore Rd, Ste 3288
Rapid City, SD 57701
www.NewHarborPress.com

Ordering Information:
Quantity sales. Special discounts are available on quantity purchases by corporations, associations, and others. For details, contact the "Special Sales Department" at the address above.

I Am / Jim Taylor. —1st ed.
ISBN 978-1-63357-441-0

This book is dedicated to Jerry and Susan Smith, for all they have done for Judy and me, And to Tim Masterson who suggested I write on this subject.

Other Books by Jim Taylor

REVELATION TO JOHN'S APOCALYPSE
UNVEILED AND REVEALED
The Spiritual View of a Carnal War

LEVITICUS UNVEILED AND REVEALED
The Lamb and the Altar — The Lamb of God and
the Cross

THE POWER OF THE CROSS UNVEILED
AND REVEALED IN JESUS
One Man Sinned and all Men Died, another Man
Died so all Might Live (Romans 5:12-21)

ALMIGHTY JEHOVAH GOD UNVEILED AND
REVEALED IN JESUS

HEBREWS UNVEILED AND REVEALED
Leviticus Fulfilled by the Coming of Jesus

Contents

About This Book

THIS BOOK IS ABOUT Jesus, the great "*I AM.*" He was the Christ child who was born to the virgin Mary, God was his birth father, and Joseph was his adoptive father. When Jesus grew into manhood, and after his resurrection, he became the King of kings, the Lord of lords, and the Savior of the world, and the cross became his throne of grace and mercy.

IN THE OLD TESTAMENT, before God became the covenant God of Israel, his chosen nation, he was known as *God Almighty*. His nation, the children of Israel, had its beginning by seventy-five souls, the descendants of Abraham, Isaac, and Jacob, all moving to Egypt to avoid starvation; it was a threatening force against all mankind, and it was caused by a sever famine that had taken over the world. After God's children had been in Egypt for several years, Pharoah took them into captivity and made them a slave nation. After 430 years of bondage to the

Pharaohs, God needed someone to deliver his children from their bondage, and that is when God met Moses; and he met him after he had been living in the wilderness for forty years. Moses had been born and raised in Egypt, and he lived in Egypt for forty years; he was forced to leave Egypt and flee to the desert to escape punishment for killing an Egyptian.

God met Moses by calling him to a burning bush that was not consumed by the fire. It was at that time *God Almighty* became known as "*I AM,*" the root word for *Jehovah.* The Spirit wrote, "And God spoke unto Moses, and said unto him, I am Jehovah: and I appeared unto Abraham, unto Isaac, and unto Jacob, as God Almighty; but by my name Jehovah I was not known to them" (Exodus 6:2-3). After *God Almighty* became the covenant God of Israel, he was known as the great "*I AM,*" or *Jehovah,* but only Israel knew him by that covenant name.

When Jehovah commanded Moses to go back to Egypt and deliver Israel from bondage to Pharoah, Moses was reluctant, but he decided it best he go as the "*I AM*" had commanded him. Moses asked God: When I speak to the elders of Israel and I tell them I have come to deliver them from their bondage, *who shall I tell them sent me?* The Spirit wrote in Exodus,

And Moses said unto God, Behold, when I come unto the children of Israel, and shall say unto them, The God of your fathers hath sent me unto you; and they shall say to me, What is his name? What shall I say unto them? And God said unto Moses, I AM THAT I AM: and he said, Thus shalt thou say unto the children of Israel, I AM hath sent me unto you. (Exodus 3:13-14)

God created Israel to become his nation, and later his kingdom, and he used Egypt as their place of isolation and refuge from the world to accomplish his purpose. The children of Abraham, Isaac, and Jacob went to Egypt as friends of the ruler of Egypt, in fact he was their brother, and his name was Joseph; but they did not know that until Joseph revealed himself to them as the one that many years earlier they had sold as a slave. But as time progressed, they became a slave people, and they were in bondage to Pharoah for 430 years. During that time they became the greatest and most powerful nation on earth, and they would soon be called, the kingdom of God.

It was many years later that Jehovah came into the world as a man by being born of a virgin, born under his own law (Galatians 4:4). He was born the Son of man, and the Son of God, and he again called himself by another name: he called himself *the Messiah* (Hebrew) or *the Christ* (Greek), both names meaning *the Anointed One*; and it is he, the Christ, who is the covenant God of the Christians, just as Jehovah was the covenant God of Israel.

The Christ's adoptive father, Joseph, and his mother, Mary, were commanded to name their Son *Jesus (Savior)*, and he would be called *Immanuel, (God with us)*. Matthew wrote,

> And she shall bring forth a son; and thou shalt call his name JESUS; for it is he that shall save his people from their sins. Now all this is come to pass, that it might be fulfilled which was spoken by the Lord

> through the prophet, saying, Behold, the virgin shall be with child, and shall bring forth a son, And they shall call his name Immanuel; which is, being interpreted, God with us. (Matthew 1:21-23)

When the great "*I AM*" became the Son of man by being born to Mary and Joseph, he became known as Christ Jesus to the Christians, and he became the "*I AM*" to them in many ways that are so very important to God's children for their security, their happiness, and the new eternal life they have with him in the kingdom of heaven.

Jesus said to his disciples, *I AM* the way, *I AM* the truth, *I AM* the life, *I AM* the resurrection, *I AM* the door, *I AM* the good Shepherd, *I AM* the light of the world, *I AM* the bread of life, *I AM* the water of Life; and he became the *I AM* in many more ways. Jesus' promises to his children were true and reliable, but when Jesus became the fulfillment of those promises himself, he certified to his children that God's promises to them were confirmed and secured by the integrity of the Almighty himself.

This book explains what each of those "*I AM*" ways mean to the Christians. When Jesus said, "I AM the way, and the truth, and the life: no one cometh unto the Father, but by me" (John 14:6), it is quite evident that he is the one and only Way to God, the Father, and he is the only Way the Christians can have life—eternal life—with him and his Father in the kingdom of heaven. When Jesus said, "I AM the resurrection, and the life: he that believeth on me, though he die, yet shall he live" it becomes clear that it is only through Jesus and his resurrection that the Christians' bodies shall be raised from their graves and given new, perfect, spiritual life in a new spiritual world. The resurrection of the saints is made infallible by the resurrection of Jesus, and his resurrection makes the saint's resurrection a fact, not just a promise. God wants his children to be assured that the promises he has made to them are certain and secure, and they cannot fail. The Hebrew author wrote,

> For when God made promise to Abraham, since he could swear by none greater, he sware by himself, saying, Surely blessing I will bless thee, and multiplying I will multiply thee. And thus, having patiently endured, he obtained the promise. For men swear by the greater: and in every dispute of theirs the oath is final for confirmation. Wherein God, being minded to show more abundantly unto the heirs of the promise the immutability of his counsel, interposed with an oath; that by two immutable things, in which it is impossible for God to lie, we may have a strong encouragement, who have fled for refuge to lay hold of the hope set before us: which we have as an anchor of the soul, a hope both sure and stedfast and entering into that which is within the veil. (Hebrews 6:13-19)

The two immutable things that secure the Christians' hope of their resurrection, and their eternal life, are *the promises God made to them,* and *those promises being se-cured and made infallible by his oath,* an oath that God swore by himself, and on his own integrity.

The most beautiful name in the world is the name of Jesus: *He is my everything, he is my all.*

Just as *Jehovah* was the covenant God of Israel, Jesus is the Christians' covenant God, and his covenant with them is: "Be thou faithful unto death, and I will give thee the crown of life" (Revelation 2:10).

Summed up, as Jehovah was the covenant God of the nation of Israel, his chosen people; and his covenant with them was to give them the fertile land of Palestine and bless them in every way as his chosen nation—Jesus is the covenant God of Christians, the church, his chosen people, and his covenant with them is to give them the kingdom of heaven—forever—in a new spiritual world. Luke wrote, "Yet seek ye his kingdom, and these things shall be added unto you. Fear not, little flock; for it is your Father's good pleasure to give you the kingdom" (Luke 12:31-32). Have you ever owned a kingdom? Would you like to? This is the place to start.

PREFACE

"*I AM*" IS THE greatest, the most powerful, and the most beautiful word recorded in the Bible. Why? There are several reasons: First, because it was the great "*I AM*" who wrote the Bible. From the first words in Genesis, "*In the beginning...*" to the last word in Revelation, "*Amen,*" every word written in the Bible was the exact word chosen by the Holy Spirit to compose his message, the Bible, and the Holy Spirit is the great "*I AM.*" He wrote those words to mean exactly what they say. It was the prophets of God who transcribed those words on paper (papaya) for all mankind to read.

THE BIBLE IS THE only source of information we have about the great "*I AM,*" whose name is Jehovah; and the book he wrote is all about Himself, the one who wrote it, and it alone tells us who he is, what he does, and the way His creation came into being. The Bible tells us when God created the world, how he created it, why he created it, and how he wants his children, whom he has given life in his own image (Genesis 1:26), to live in it. The Bible is the Christians' instruction Book that tells them how they should properly use all the good things God has richly given them to enjoy (1 Timothy 6:17).

The Bible is so very important because it alone contains the history of how sin came into the world through just one man, Adam (Romans 5:12-21; 1 Corinthians 15:21-22), and how that one transgression brought sin and death into the world and condemned everything God made—and broke God's heart in the process (Genesis 6:6-7). The Bible contains the record of what the great *"I AM"* must accomplish to keep his word in either judging and destroying his creation because of Adam's transgression or redeeming it. God's love for his new world and for his children was so great it would not allow him to destroy it, with all his children, and so he chose to redeem it. He did so at infinite cost to himself; it cost God his only begotten Son's life to redeem the creation and restore it back into its original beauty, glory, and perfection—and all of that shall be accomplished to perfection (2 Peter 3:11-13) because of the great price Jesus paid to achieve it. Peter spoke of the infinite price God paid to redeem his creation when he wrote,

> And if ye call on him as Father, who without respect of persons judgeth according to each man's work, pass the time of your sojourning in fear: knowing that ye were redeemed, not with corruptible things, with silver or gold, from your vain manner

of life handed down from your fathers; but with precious blood, as of a lamb without spot, even the blood of Christ: who was foreknown indeed before the foundation of the world, but was manifested at the end of the times for your sake, who through him are believers in God, that raised him from the dead, and gave him glory; so that your faith and hope might be in God. (1 Peter 1:17-21)

Peter also wrote of how that shall all be accomplished, and what the result will be of all that Jesus achieved in his work of redemption.

The Lord is not slack concerning his promise, as some count slackness; but is longsuffering to you-ward, not wishing that any should perish, but that all should come to repentance. But the day of the Lord will come as a thief; in the which the heavens shall pass away with a great noise, and the elements shall be dissolved with fervent heat, and the earth and the works that are therein shall be burned up. Seeing that these things are thus all to be dissolved, what manner of persons ought ye to be in all holy living and godliness, looking for and earnestly desiring the coming of the day of God, by reason of which the heavens being on fire shall be dissolved, and the elements shall melt with fervent

> heat? But, according to his promise, we
> look for new heavens and a new earth,
> wherein dwelleth righteousness. (2 Peter
> 3:9-13)

There are some who would die for another; a father might die for a son, a husband for his wife (Romans 5:6-8); but who would sacrifice the life of *their only son* to save the life of any other? It appears that God our heavenly Father is the only one who would do that. Therefore, who suffered the most when the Word left heaven to enter the fallen world he had created, and he become the Son of man who would offer his life on a cross, as a ransom (Matthew 20:28), to take away the sins of the word? Was it the Father who had to witness his Son's sufferings, or was it Jesus who suffered? When Jesus was in the garden of Gethsemane pleading for his life, praying to his Father he would not have to endure the cross, what were his Father's feelings when he heard his Son's prayer, but he must deny his request?

> Then cometh Jesus with them unto a
> place called Gethsemane, and saith unto
> his disciples, Sit ye here, while I go yonder and pray. And he took with him Peter
> and the two sons of Zebedee, and began
> to be sorrowful and sore troubled. Then
> saith he unto them, My soul is exceeding
> sorrowful, even unto death: abide ye here,
> and watch with me. And he went forward
> a little, and fell on his face, and prayed,
> saying, My Father, if it be possible, let this

cup pass away from me: nevertheless, not as I will, but as thou wilt. And he cometh unto the disciples, and findeth them sleeping, and saith unto Peter, What, could ye not watch with me one hour? Watch and pray, that ye enter not into temptation: the spirit indeed is willing, but the flesh is weak. Again a second time he went away, and prayed, saying, My Father, if this cannot pass away, except I drink it, thy will be done. And he came again and found them sleeping, for their eyes were heavy. And he left them again, and went away, and prayed a third time, saying again the same words. (Matthew 26:36-44)

The Father paid an infinite price to redeem the creation from certain annihilation and blot out all the sins of the world when he told his son—*NO! You must drink the cup*! It was there in the garden, where Jesus' prayed, that his Father accepted his soul as an offering for sin (Isaiah 53:10), and he saw the travail of his soul (Isaiah 53:11), and was satisfied that the offering Jesus was making to save the creation from sin, death, and annihilation was of much greater value than was the creation itself, and therefore the world God created was saved. Paul wrote,

For the earnest expectation of the creation waiteth for the revealing of the sons of God. For the creation was subjected to vanity, not of its own will, but by reason of him who subjected it, in hope that the creation itself also shall be delivered from the bondage of corruption into the liberty of the glory of the children of God. For we know that the whole creation groaneth and travaileth in pain together until now. (Romans 8:19-21)

The price the Word himself paid to forgive all sinners and redeem the creation from annihilation was to wash their sins away by the blood of His cross. John wrote, "If we say that we have fellowship with him and walk in the darkness, we lie, and do not the truth: but if we walk in the light, as he is in the light, we have fellowship one with another, and the blood of Jesus his Son cleanseth us from all sin" (1 John 1:6-7). The Word, who is God (John 1:1-2), was made flesh (John 1:14) to qualify himself to be *the Man* who would offer his life on the cross as a perfect human sacrifice that truly indeed would take away the sins of the world (John 1:29).

The great *"I AM"* also became a man so he could fill the office of the High Priest, the only One who was sanctioned to offer his sacrifice to God (Hebrews 5:1). To become that man he gave up his equality with God (Philippians 2:5-8), and he became a man in all points like all other men (Hebrews 2:17). The man he became was called Jesus, the Christ.

Jesus was in a continual process of paying the price necessary to redeem the creation from annihilation from the day he was born to Mary until the day he was resurrected and received back into heaven in glory. Paul wrote, "And without controversy great is the mystery of godliness; He who was manifested in the flesh, Justified in the Spirit, seen of angels, Preached among the nations, Believed on in the world, Received up in glory" (1 Timothy 3:16).

The man Jesus became suffered many things that are beyond comprehension so he could qualify himself to pay the price necessary to become the perfect sin offering that truly would save the creation from annihilation. Paul wrote, "Him who knew no sin he made to be sin on our behalf; that we might become the righteousness of God in him" (2 Corinthians 5:21). It was Jesus, the Son of God, who was willing to be made sin, the very thing he despised more than death itself, so when he was nailed to the cross, sin also was nailed to the cross, and when he died on the cross, sin died with him.

The sacrifice Jesus offered on the cross was infinitely more than sufficient than what was necessary to restore all the things that had been defiled by sin back into their original glory and perfection (Acts 3:18-21), and of much greater value than what was necessary to forgive all sinners and put away all the sins of the world. A believing person shall be forgiven instantly of all their sins the moment they are baptized (Mark 16:16; Acts 2:38; 22:16), and they can maintain their salvation for the rest of their lives by their faith (Revelation 2:10).

The reason that is all accomplished so perfectly and so quickly is because of the value of the sacrifice that was offered to accomplish it—the very life blood of the Son of God.

Not only is the Word *"I AM"* the most beautiful Word, the greatest Word, and the most powerful word in the Bible, but it is also a difficult Word to understand, and very difficult to translate. No language can be translated into another language without some loss, some gain, or some difference. That is just the way it is. The Word *"I*

AM" can best be understood by describing Someone who has no beginning, who is, and who will always be forever, without end. The Hebrew author said it best in his narrative of Jesus in just a few words when he wrote, "Jesus Christ is the same yesterday and to-day, (yea) and for ever" (Hebrews 13:8).

It was God who named himself the *"I AM,"* and that occurred when he called Moses, who had been living in the wilderness for forty years, to view a burning bush that was not consumed by the fire. When Moses approached the bush to see why it was not consumed, he was told to take off his shoes, *for he was standing on holy ground*—for that bush was the living God, the great *"I AM."* It was at that moment God became known to Moses, and to Israel, as *Jehovah, the great "I AM,"* for that was the time when God chose that name to identify himself as the Holy Covenant God of Israel. The Spirit wrote, "And God spoke unto Moses, and said unto him, I am Jehovah: and I appeared unto Abraham, unto Isaac, and unto Jacob, as God Almighty; but by my name Jehovah I was not known to them" (Exodus 6:2-3). The word *"I AM"* is the root word for the name *Jehovah*; he who was and had no beginning, he who is, and he who shall always be, for he is the eternal One.

Jehovah called Moses to his bush to command him to return to Egypt and deliver his children, the Israelites, out of Egyptian bondage. Moses was the only man God had who was qualified to accomplish such a task. First, he had been born an Israelite in the tribe of Levi, and he knew Israel's language and Israel's ways and customs, but he had been brought up in Pharoah's palace, and he was raised by Pharoah's daughter (Exodus 2:1-10). Therefore, he also knew Egypt, the Egyptian language, the Egyptian culture, and Pharoah, the king. However, *Moses' nursemaid was his own mother*, and she taught him who he was, and Israelite, why he had been born, and what his mission was; *Moses' task was to deliver Israel from bondage to Pharoah.*

When Moses was forty years of age, he decided to visit his people, Israel. Maybe he thought he would accomplish the task his mother taught him he was born to achieve. He saw an Israelite being abused by and Egyptian and he killed and buried the Egyptian. When that incident was revealed to Pharoah, Moses had to flee Egypt (Exodus 2:11-15). He lived another forty years in the desert, during which time he learned how to live and survive in the wilderness. It was those attributes that qualified Moses to deliver Israel from Egyptian bondage, and no other man on earth stood in his shoes. However, Moses decided he was not going to return to Egypt, and he would have nothing to do with facing Pharoah. Moses told God he was not going, send someone else. God said, *I want you*! Moses told God he had tried to deliver Israel from bondage forty years ago and he suffered greatly for his mistake—find someone else!—*I am not going*! God said, *we shall see about that*! Moses went (Exodus 4:20).

Moses had a question: He asked God; when the children of Israel ask me why I came to them to attempt such an impossible task as to save them from their slavery, *Who shall I say sent me*? The Spirit wrote,

And Moses said unto God, Behold, when I come unto the children of Israel, and shall say unto them, The God of your fathers hath sent me unto you; and they shall say to me, What is his name? What shall I say unto them? And God said unto Moses, I AM THAT I AM: and he said, Thus shalt thou say unto the children of Israel, I AM hath sent me unto you. (Exodus 3:13-14)

It was the *"I AM"* who called Moses to his burning bush, and it was he who many years later left the Godhead to become the Son of man—His name is Jesus. When God needed someone to deliver his children out of bondage to Pharoah, he sent a man, his name was Moses. When God needed someone to deliver his children out of sin and death, he sent no one. *He came Himself.*

Another reason the word *"I AM"* is so great is because he is the One who created the world and gave life to all living creatures. Life must come from preexisting life, it cannot be created by men, it must be given by the One *who is life*, and who has always been life, and his name is Jesus. John wrote, "In him was life; and the life was the light of men" (John 1:4). Paul wrote, "So also it is written, The first man Adam became a living soul. The last Adam became a life-giving spirit" (1 Corinthians 15:45).

It was only mankind, humans, who were created very special, for they alone were created in the image of God. The Spirit wrote,

> And God said, Let us make man in our im-age, after our likeness: and let them have dominion over the fish of the sea, and over the birds of the heavens, and over the cattle, and over all the earth, and over

every creeping thing that creepeth upon
the earth. (Genesis 1:26)

Not only were men created in the image of God, who
is the Father of their spirits (Hebrews 12:9), *but God's
children were given the entire creation as his gift to them!*
God's children were to own the creation and have complete control over it, and everything in it! When God
created his new world, the new creation, the kingdom
of heaven—just as God gave Adam the original creation,
he gave the Christians his new creation, the kingdom
of God—*it is God's children, the Christians, who own the
kingdom of heaven.* Luke wrote, "Yet seek ye his kingdom,
and these things shall be added unto you. Fear not, little
flock; for it is your Father's good pleasure to give you the
kingdom" (Luke 12:31-32). The Word of God, the Bible,
is the only source of information we have that explains
how all of that transpired, and it is also the instruction
Book the "*I AM*" wrote to his children to educate them in
the way they were required to live in his new world.

There are many people who do not believe in God. The
Psalmist wrote, "The fool hath said in his heart, There is
no God. They are corrupt, they have done abominable
works; There is none that doeth good" (Psalms 14:1;
53:1). Paul wrote that there is no excuse for not believing in the Almighty. He said,

> For the wrath of God is revealed from
> heaven against all ungodliness and unrigh-
> teousness of men, who hinder the truth
> in unrighteousness; because that which
> is known of God is manifest in them; for

God manifested it unto them. For the invisible things of him since the creation of the world are clearly seen, being perceived through the things that are made, even his everlasting power and divinity; that they may be without excuse" (Romans 1:18-20).

Paul wrote that when God created the world and all mankind, he put into his children's minds *the fact that He is*, that He is the great "*I AM*," and he is the Creator and Life-giver of all the living, and there is no excuse for failing to believe in him; that He is the Almighty—that is all instinctive knowledge that is self-evident. Even the Declaration of Independence written by Thomas Jefferson established that, when he said, We consider these trues to be *self-evident*, that all men are created equal. The creation, and all that is in it; the things we see, the things we feel, and the things we hear, and to view the conception and birth of a baby from their beginning to the birth all prove that it had to have been designed, created, built, and organized into what we have today; it is all the works of God and his creation that clearly establish his existence. If a person found something as simple as a glove he would have to know that glove had been made, or manufactured by someone, or it could not exist. But which is more complex, the glove or the hand that is in the glove? Did the hand have no designer and creator? The Hebrew writer said, "And without faith it is impossible to be well-pleasing unto him; for he that cometh to

God must believe that he is, and that he is a rewarder of them that seek after him" (Hebrews 11:6).

What would be the consequences of there not being a Creator, a God who in the beginning made this world and everything in in? The only logical conclusion is, *there just would not be anything here;* there would be no world, no universe, no space—*nothing!* There are two things, maybe more, that are impossible for the human mind to comprehend. One is eternal, something that has no beginning, and has no end. When we try to understand the very beginning of something the question that comes to mind is, *What was there before that?* The other thing beyond understanding is *nothing.* Exactly, *what is nothing?* When we hear strange noises coming from our children's room, and we ask, "*What are you doing in there?*" and they say, "*Nothing,*" we immediately investigate. The view this author has of *nothing* is—*it is the absence of everything.* It would be to go to the farthest outreach of space and far away from the most remote star and cut out one cubic meter of space and remove it from its place. According to what this author has read there is one molecule of substance, or mass, in every cubic meter of space, unknown as to what element it might be. Then the article concluded by saying there is more mass in space than is contained in all the stars, all the planets, and all the galaxies.

But if one cubic meter of space was cut out of its place and removed, what would be left there? The only possible answer is, *nothing;* but is that a true answer? That empty place where that cubic meter of space had just been is still there. And so it will be with all the creation when God rolls up space like a mantle (Hebrews 1:10-12), and it is dissolved in fervent heat (2 Peter 3:10) —what will be there where the universe had been? It is impossible to understand *nothing,* or to comprehend what was here before God created the universe, or what will be left here, *nothing,* when space is rolled up like a mantle, or a carpet (Hebrews 1:10-12), and burned. Peter wrote,

> but the heavens that now are, and the earth, by the same word have been stored up for fire, being reserved against the day of judgment and destruction of ungodly men...But the day of the Lord will come as a thief; in the which the heavens shall pass away with a great noise, and the elements shall be dissolved with fervent heat, and the earth and the works that are therein shall be burned up. Seeing that these things are thus all to be dissolved, what manner of persons ought ye to be in all holy living and godliness, looking for and earnestly desiring the coming of the day of God, by reason of which the heavens being on fire shall be dissolved, and the elements shall melt with fervent heat? But, according to his promise, we look for new heavens and a new earth, wherein dwelleth righteousness. (2 Peter 3:7-13)

According to Peter, when this creation is destroyed it will be the new heavens and the new earth that will replace it.

A person who believes in evolution (Darwin's evolution) believes space and mass have always been here. They start their theory by believing life came from mud, a lightning strike, and amoebas. But even space is a created substance, and it was created by God for him to have a place to put things—like the sun, the moon, the stars, and the earth. Read it, "In the beginning God created *the heavens* and the earth...." (Genesis 1:1). After God created the stars he counted them and called them by their names (Psalms 147:4-5).

Before space was created, what was there that subsisted? And when space is removed and rolled up like a mantle (Hebrews 1:10-12), what will be there in its place? Where did the stars come from? They are complex nuclear power sources that are fueled by nuclear energy, and as such they could not have just suddenly come into their own existence and have been burning forever—they had to have had a beginning, they had to have been designed, and then they were created—and they are burning themselves out of existence by consuming the nuclear energy of which they consist. The sun, our star that lights and heats the earth is burning itself out at the rate of 4,000 pounds of nuclear energy every second. How much longer will it last? Given enough time it will burn out and suffer a heat death.

The Hebrew author wrote,

> And, Thou, Lord, in the beginning didst lay the foundation of the earth, And the heavens are the works of thy hands: They shall perish; but thou continuest: And they

all shall wax old as doth a garment; And
as a mantle shalt thou roll them up, As a
garment, and they shall be changed: But
thou art the same, And thy years shall not
fail. (Hebrews 1:10-12)

It is impossible to comprehend space being rolled up
like a mantle and there being nothing left in its place.
It also is not possible to understand what Peter wrote
that the heavens that now are (space) are reserved to be
burned with intense fire. Can space burn? A person who
does not believe in God, and that he is the Creator of all
things, including life, has many questions to answer that
without God have no answer.

When Adam (and all men) sinned against God
(Romans 5:12, 19), and condemned everything God created, it was the *"I AM"* who came to redeem it. To accomplish that, the Almighty himself left his Most Holy Place
in heaven and gave up his equality with God (Philippians
2:5-8) to become a man in all points just like all other
men (Hebrews 2:17). That happened when Mary gave
birth to Jesus. God accomplished everything necessary
to redeem his creation from sin and death by becoming
a man and sacrificing himself to save it, and his name is
Jesus.

Jesus lived in the world as all men must live in it, and
he was tempted in all points just as all other men are
tempted (Hebrews 4:15), and even more: When he was
tempted in the garden to not go through with his death
on the cross, his crucifixion (Matthew 26:38-39), he was
tempted more severely than any other man could ever be

tempted. Jesus could have called upon his own deity for the power and strength, *and the right*, to just rise up and walk right out of that place. But he didn't! And that is the reason we have been saved from sin and death and given eternal life.

It was by God's own choice that he became the Son of man to offer himself as a sacrifice to take away the sins of the world. That was the only way that God could punish sin with death, as he promised he would do, by dying himself in the place of all sinners to save his creation—and all men from—from annihilation. Jesus died the death all other men deserved to die because they were sinners—and he died to take away their sins, and all the sins of the world (John 1:29). Consider that Sacrifice! When the Almighty *"I AM"* lived in his Most Holy Place in heaven he would not allow himself to be seen by men—upon the pain of death! (Exodus 33:20). No one, not even an angel could approach God in his Holy Place—unless they had been invited. That is our God who is love (1 John 4:8, 16); however, he is also a consuming fire (Hebrews 12:29). His love for us and his creation is so intense that if overwhelmed his holiness, and he was willing to become a man to be seen, gazed at, handled, beaten, spit on, scourged, crowned with thorns, and crucified—far from the life he lived and the protection he had when he occupied his Most Holy Place in heaven. At the end of Jesus' life he was forsaken by God, His Father, to pay the price that was demanded to take away the sins of the world—sins that other men had committed (Isaiah 53:8; Matthew 27:46). That was the necessary punishment he must suffer to save his creation from annihilation and redeem all men from sin and death—and he paid that price on the cross.

That all occurred when Jesus was cut off out of the land of the living (Isaiah 53:8), and he voluntarily went into the forbidden place of the dead, Hades, *but he was promised by his Father he would not be left there* (Acts 2:30-32, ASV). Having given up his equality with God he had no other escape from that horrible place than by trusting the promises of his Father. Jesus was cut off out of the land of the living (Isaiah 53:8) he poured out his soul unto death (Isaiah 53:12), and God saw the travail of his soul and was satisfied (Isaiah 53:11). But by the resurrection Jesus' body, soul, and spirit were all once again made alive. Peter wrote, "Because Christ also suffered for sins once, the righteous for the unrighteous, that he might bring us to God; being put to death in the flesh, but made alive in the spirit; in which also he went and preached unto the spirits in prison" (1 Peter 3:18-19). That is the time when Jesus' soul, and the travail of his soul were made an offering for sin. Isaiah wrote,

> By oppression and judgment he was taken away; and as for his generation, who among them considered that he was cut off out of the land of the living for the transgression of my people to whom the stroke was due? And they made his grave with the wicked, and with a rich man in his death; although he had done no violence, neither was any deceit in his mouth. Yet it pleased Jehovah to bruise him; he hath

put him to grief: when thou shalt make his soul an offering for sin, he shall see his seed, he shall prolong his days, and the pleasure of Jehovah shall prosper in his hand. He shall see of the travail of his soul, and shall be satisfied: by the knowledge of himself shall my righteous servant justify many; and he shall bear their iniquities. Therefore will I divide him a portion with the great, and he shall divide the spoil with the strong; because he poured out his soul unto death, and was numbered with the transgressors: yet he bare the sin of many, and made intercession for the transgressors. (Isaiah 53:8-12)

INTRODUCTION

JESUS CAME INTO THE world just like all other men enter it; he was born of a woman, born under the law (Galatians 4:3-5)—with two exceptions, his mother was a virgin (Isaiah 7:14) and God was his birth Father. When Jesus was very young, he knew he was the Son of God, and he knew his Father had sent him into the world to be its Savior. He knew the Law of Moses, and he knew he was required to keep that law perfectly throughout his entire life—it was the law that he, himself had given to Moses. He knew he would end his life by being crucified, and that he would offer his perfect life to God as a human sacrifice that truly was sufficient to take away the sins of the world (John 1:29). He had that knowledge when he was only twelve years of age (Luke 2:41-52). That will be discussed below. That is something for him to have live with for his entire life; to know how, and when he was going to die.

When Jesus was born it was necessary for him to have parents to raise him, to support him, and to teach him the things that were necessary for him to live and survive in this present world. Mary was the name of the young virgin who was to become the mother of God's Son, Jesus, and his father (his adoptive father) was called Joseph, but his birth Father was God. Jesus was born into the world he created, and he was born under the Law of Moses; the law he had established.

What must Mary have thought when Gabriel the arch angel appeared to her, and He did not ask her, but he told her she was the one whom God had chosen to become the mother of his child? The child's father would be Jehovah God himself, and Joseph would be his father to raise him. Mary and Joseph were to name their child *JESUS* (Matthew 1:21). Could any woman (or man) even begin to imagine what an experience like the one written below would cause a person to feel? Luke wrote,

> Now in the sixth month the angel Gabriel was sent from God unto a city of Galilee, named Nazareth, to a virgin betrothed to a man whose name was Joseph, of the house of David; and the virgin's name was Mary. And he came in unto her, and said, Hail, thou that art highly favored, the Lord is with thee. But she was greatly troubled at the saying, and cast in her mind what manner of salutation this might be. And the angel said unto her, Fear not, Mary: for thou hast found favor with God. And

behold, thou shalt conceive in thy womb, and bring forth a son, and shalt call his name JESUS. He shall be great, and shall be called the Son of the Most High: and the Lord God shall give unto him the throne of his father David: and he shall reign over the house of Jacob for ever; and of his kingdom there shall be no end. And Mary said unto the angel, How shall this be, seeing I know not a man? And the angel answered and said unto her, The Holy Spirit shall come upon thee, and the power of the Most High shall overshadow thee: wherefore also the holy thing which is begotten shall be called the Son of God. And behold, Elisabeth thy kinswoman, she also hath conceived a son in her old age; and this is the sixth month with her that was called barren. For no word from God shall be void of power. And Mary said, Behold, the handmaid of the Lord; be it unto me according to thy word. And the angel departed from her. (Luke 1:26-38)

The child Mary was about to bring into the world was the Word of God, who is God, and who became flesh (John 1:14) by being born of a woman (Galatians 4:4). He was Jehovah, the Creator of the heavens and the earth, the Messiah, the Christ, who is the great "*I AM.*"

Joseph and Mary were a young couple who were about to become husband and wife. They had been chosen by

God to become the parents of his Son. They were both righteous and godly people, and they were very poor. But when Joseph found out that he was about to marry a pregnant woman, and he knew the child she was carrying was not his, he did not know what to do. He could have had her stoned for adultery (Deuteronomy 22:23–24). However, he loved Mary with a great passion, and her being pregnant greatly distressed him. Mary told Joseph the truth, that she had not been with a man, and her child had been fathered by the Holy Spirit. Mary told Joseph she was carrying God's Child, and she was going to give birth to the Son of God, the Messiah, the Christ. For some reason Joseph did not believe her. Joseph did not want to hurt Mary beyond the problems they already had, so he decided to divorce her quietly, and he was not going to give the reason why he was putting her away. By the Law of Moses he could do that (Deuteronomy 24:1). It required an angel of the Lord to appear to Joseph to convince him Mary was telling the truth, and the child she was carrying truly was the Son of God.

What other thoughts must have gone through Mary's and Joseph's minds the moment they both understood that they were the ones who had been chosen by God to be the parents of His Son? What must Joseph have thought about becoming the father of the Messiah, and it would be his duty to raise him, to feed him, to take care of him, and to give him his education? How could Joseph, a poorly educated carpenter himself, teach the Son of God, the Creator of the world, anything about life or about facing the problems he knew He would have?

How could Joseph teach Jesus, the creator of all worlds, how to use a saw, or how to hold a hammer?

Jesus was born to Joseph and Mary just as the prophets predicted he would be, and he became exactly what they said he would become, the Son of God, the Son of man, the Christ. When Mary kissed the face of her beloved Son, Jesus, did she know she was kissing the face of God?

Jesus grew and matured just as all other children grow and mature. Luke wrote "And Jesus advanced in wisdom and stature, and in favor with God and men" (Luke 2:52). When he became a man he was baptized by John (Matthew 3:13-17). He entered his ministry when he was about thirty years of age (Luke 3:23).

Until the time of Christ Israel had been God's chosen nation, and to the Jews alone were all the promises and blessings of God decreed (Psalms 147:19-20). Paul wrote, "For I am not ashamed of the gospel: for it is the power of God unto salvation to every one that believeth; to the Jew first, and also to the Greek" (Romans 1:16). Because all the promises God made concerning the establishment of the kingdom of God and the coming of the Savior were made to Israel, or to the Jews, when God sent his Son into the world he sent him to the Jews. Therefore, when Jesus came, he worked with the Jews. Jesus said he was sent only to the lost sheep of the house of Israel (Matthew 15:24). When Jesus sent his apostles out into the world to preach the Word and teach the gospel, they also were first sent only to the Jews (Matthew 10:5-7). That is called the limited commission. Paul did the same. When he began his ministry he went first to the Jews, and when they would not listen, he turned to the Gentiles (Acts 13:44-49). Paul was appointed to be the apostle to the Gentiles (Galatians 2:9).

Jesus went to the Jews and he tried to teach them, but they refused to listen to him (Matthew 13:54-58; John 6:65-69). But Jesus did not enter the world just to save Israel, he came to be Savior of all nations and all people, and therefore he pressed on to fulfill his ministry. It is strange that the time Jesus went to a Samaritan village— to people who were not Jews—all the people listened intently to everything he had to say, and he converted the whole village in just a few days (John 4:1-45).

Jesus taught his disciples that he came into the world with the definite purpose of going into Jerusalem to be chastised and abused by the religious leaders of Israel, to be beaten, spit upon, scourged, crowned with thorns, and nailed to the cross to be left to die (Matthew 16:21– 23; Mark 8:31–33; Luke 9:22, 17:24-25), and it could not be any other way (Matthew 26:51–54). Jesus said, "Now is my soul troubled; and what shall I say? Father, save me from this hour. But for this cause came I unto this hour" (John 12:27).

Just as Jesus continually taught his disciples about how he must suffer and die, and it could not be any other way, he also spoke to Joseph and Mary with the same message. He wanted to prepare his parents for the terrible day he would be crucified. There must have come a time when Joseph and Mary did not want to hear any more about the dreadful way their Son's life would end, any more than did his apostles want to hear those things (Matthew 16:21-23). However, they had no choice. Can we even imagine how many times Joseph must have told his Son that he had heard enough, and not to speak of those things any longer.

Joseph died somewhere between the year Jesus was twelve and the time he began his ministry, because the last mention of Jesus' father is in Luke 2:40–52. That was the time when Joseph, Mary, and Jesus had gone to Jerusalem to keep the Passover feast.

When Mary and Joseph left Jerusalem, after they had celebrated the Passover, Jesus stayed behind in the temple. Jesus was such a reliable and obedient child that Joseph and Mary just assumed Jesus was with them, and they were a day's journey out of Jerusalem before they realized he was not with them. Jesus was in the temple with the doctors, the lawyers, and the rulers of the synagogue, and he amazed them with his questions and answers (Luke 2:46-47). At that young age Jesus knew he was the Son of God, he knew who his real Father was, and he knew what his Father's business was—Salvation! He knew what his purpose in life would be. However, Joseph never saw Jesus accomplish his mission. When Jesus went to the cross Joseph was not there, for he had died.

God removed Joseph from this world and took him home to heaven before Jesus went to the cross. God must have known that Jesus' crucifixion was a burden Joseph could not endure to witness—he could not bear seeing his Son spit on and terribly abused, and then nailed to the cross to be lifted up and left to die. Joseph's going home to be with God was an act of great mercy on God's part to spare him from having to witness his Son's crucifixion

(Isaiah 57:1–2). God knew Joseph could never withstand the grief, the misery, the pain, and the agony that would come with seeing such a terrible thing happen to his beloved Son whom he loved dearly.

However, Mary, Jesus' mother was there when Jesus was crucified (John 19:25). She seems to have stood up strongly against the terrible thing she had to witness, seeing her beloved Son being so terribly abused and nailed to the cross to be left there until he died. Jesus must have prepared Mary well for his crucifixion by continually telling her of all the things he must suffer, and why his suffering and death on the cross were necessary. Mary, even though she had been well prepared for what must transpire, and knowing how her Son must die, could never, never be prepared to accept it without the greatest pain and agony any person must endure. However, because she had been so well prepared, she did endure it and accepted it as the will of God.

Mary treasured in her heart everything she heard concerning her Son, such as the things she heard from the shepherds during the time Jesus was born (Luke 2:16-19). If anyone knew who Jesus truly was, the Son of God, and believed every word he spoke, it was Mary. She knew only God could have planted that little seed in her womb to give life to the Messiah, God's Son, when she was still a virgin. Of all those who were standing by the cross and witnessing Jesus' crucifixion, and knew exactly what was taking place, and why Jesus had to die such a horrible death, it was his true birth Father in heaven, and Mary, his mother.

Jesus was buried in a new tomb, a tomb that belonged to Joseph of Arimathaea (Isaiah 53:9), a disciple of Jesus; and he must have prepared it for himself because it was new, and no body had ever been buried in it. John wrote, "So they took the body of Jesus, and bound it in linen cloths with the spices, as the custom of the Jews is to bury. Now in the place where he was crucified there was a garden; and in the garden a new tomb wherein was never man yet laid" (John 19:40-41). When the disciples opened the tomb, and they saw it was empty, they did not have to count bodies to see if it was Jesus' body that was missing.

It is interesting that on the Sunday morning after Jesus' crucifixion, and he had been buried, several women went to the tomb of Jesus to anoint Jesus' body (Mathew 28:1, Luke 24:1, 8-10), but Mary, Jesus' mother, was not mentioned as being one of those women who went to the tomb. *Why?* Mary believed so strongly everything Jesus told her about how he must die, why he must die, and that he would be raised from the dead on the third day—*she knew there would not be any body in that tomb to anoint.*

CHAPTER 1

"*I AM*" JESUS — ALMIGHTY JEHOVAH GOD

WHEN JESUS TAUGHT THE people about who he was, where he had come from, and why he came, they refused to believe him. Jesus claimed he came from God (John 8:42) and that he was the Son of God (John 19:7), and he worked great miracles to prove he was telling the truth. But those to whom he came, the Jews, could not see any difference in him, who he was, and who they were, and they were offended in him. Mathew wrote,

> And it came to pass, when Jesus had finished these parables, he departed thence. And coming into his own country he taught them in their synagogue,

insomuch that they were astonished, and said, Whence hath this man this wisdom, and these mighty works? is not this the carpenter's son? is not his mother called Mary? and his brethren, James, and Joseph, and Simon, and Judas? And his sisters, are they not all with us? Whence then hath this man all these things? And they were offended in him. But Jesus said unto them, A prophet is not without honor, save in his own country, and in his own house. And he did not many mighty works there because of their unbelief. (Matthew 13:53-57)

Instead of the Jews questioning Jesus' wisdom and his ability to perform great miracles, they should have quickly understood that he truly was sent by his Father just as he claimed, or he could not accomplish the works he performed. Instead, their prejudiced minds did not permit them such reasoning, and so they attacked him for accomplishing things they just could not believe were possible.

It was Jesus' works, what he taught, and who he claimed to be that caused him to be nailed to the cross and left to die. Jesus claimed to be equal to the Father, and that he was the Father, but the Jews would not accept that, so they took up stones to stone him for blasphemy. John wrote,

Jesus said to him, I am the Way, and the Truth, and the Life. No one comes to the

Father except through Me. If you had known Me, you would have known My Father also; and from now on you do know Him, and have seen Him. And Philip said to Him, Lord, show us the Father, and it is enough for us. Jesus said to him, Am I so long a time with you, and you have not known Me, Philip? The one seeing Me has seen the Father! And how do you say, Show us the Father? Do you not believe that I am in the Father and the Father is in Me? The Words which I speak to you I do not speak from Myself, but the Father who abides in Me, He does the works. Believe Me that I am in the Father, and the Father is in Me; but if not, believe Me because of the works themselves. (John 14:6-11)

My sheep hear my voice, and I know them, and they follow me: and I give unto them eternal life; and they shall never perish, and no one shall snatch them out of my hand. My Father, who hath given them unto me, is greater than all; and no one is able to snatch them out of the Father's hand. I and the Father are one. The Jews took up stones again to stone him. Jesus answered them, Many good works have I showed you from the Father; for which of those works do ye stone me? The Jews answered him, For a good work we stone

thee not, but for blasphemy; and because
that thou, being a man, makest thyself
God. (John 10:27-33)

Jesus taught that he and the Father were One, and that
he, himself, was the great *"I AM."* In making such a statement he claimed to be Jehovah, the Israelites' mighty and
holy God. If Jesus were not speaking the truth then he
was blaspheming, for the name *Jehovah* was such a holy
name to the Israelites that they would not write it or
speak it. That is why the Jews picked up stones to stone
him, for stoning was the Jewish penalty for blasphemy.
But when Jesus could prove by the miracles he worked
that everything he taught was the truth, they should have
believed him. Jesus said, "But the witness which I have is
greater than that of John; for the works which the Father
hath given me to accomplish, the very works that I do,
bear witness of me, that the Father hath sent me" (John
5:36). "If I do not the works of my Father, believe me
not. But if I do them, though ye believe not me, believe
the works: that ye may know and understand that the
Father is in me, and I in the Father" (John 10:37-38).

When Moses was serving God by agreeing to go to
Egypt to deliver Israel out of his bondage, he was continually given instructions from the Almighty as exactly
what to do and how to do it. It came to the point Moses
wanted more than to just hear his words, he wanted to
see the One he was serving, and to know more about
him, just as Thomas wanted to see the Father. Jehovah
said to Moses: Moses, no one can see my face, no one can
see my glory and live (Exodus 33:12-23). If Moses could

have lived another 1,600 years his request would have been granted, for anyone who looked upon Jesus was seeing Jehovah, God Almighty, face to face and in his glory, for he who has seen Jesus has seen the Father, for Jesus was the Father (John 14:7-11, 10:30).

There were other things Jesus taught that caused him grievous problems because they not only sounded too good to be true, they appeared to be impossible. Jesus taught his Jewish brethren that if they would believe in him and keep his Word they would never see of death. John wrote,

> Verily, verily, I say unto you, If a man keep my word, he shall never see death. The Jews said unto him, Now we know that thou hast a demon. Abraham died, and the prophets; and thou sayest, If a man keep my word, he shall never taste of death. Art thou greater than our father Abraham, who died? and the prophets died: whom makest thou thyself? Jesus answered, If I glorify myself, my glory is nothing: it is my Father that glorifieth me; of whom ye say, that he is your God; and ye have not known him: but I know him; and if I should say, I know him not, I shall be like unto you, a liar: but I know him, and keep his word. Your father Abraham rejoiced to see my day; and he saw it, and was glad. The Jews therefore said unto him, Thou art not yet fifty years old, and

hast thou seen Abraham? Jesus said unto them, Verily, verily, I say unto you, Before Abraham was born, I AM. They took up stones therefore to cast at him: but Jesus hid himself, and went out of the temple. (John 8:51-59)

The Old Testament is very clear in revealing that the one who was going to come into the world as the Messiah would be Jehovah Himself. Jeremiah wrote,

Behold, the days come, saith Jehovah, that I will raise unto David a righteous Branch, and he shall reign as king and deal wisely, and shall execute justice and righteousness in the land. In his days Judah shall be saved, and Israel shall dwell safely; and this is his name whereby he shall be called: Jehovah our righteousness. (Jeremiah 23:5-6)

The righteous Branch from David can be none other than Jesus, the Son of David (Matthew 1:1). He was not only the Branch of David—he was also David's Root. When Jesus spoke to the seven churches of Asia, in John's revelation letter, he said, "I Jesus have sent mine angel to testify unto you these things for the churches. I am the root and the offspring of David, the bright, the morning star" (Revelation 22:16). It is that nature of Jesus that confounded the Pharisees, and they wanted him to say something, anything, so they could convict him of blasphemy and stone him. So, they ask Jesus many questions to try to deceive him in his speech. They wanted him to say something they could use against him. But Jesus' answers were so precise that the Pharisees did not know how to respond to them, and so they quit asking him questions. Matthew wrote,

> Then went the Pharisees, and took counsel how they might ensnare him in his talk. And they send to him their disciples, with the Herodians, saying, Teacher, we know that thou art true, and teachest the way of God in truth, and carest not for any one: for thou regardest not the person of men. Tell us therefore, What thinkest thou? Is it lawful to give tribute unto Caesar, or not? But Jesus perceived their wickedness, and said, Why make ye trial of me, ye hypocrites? Show me the tribute money. And they brought unto him a denarius. And he saith unto them, Whose is this image and superscription? They say unto him, Caesar's. Then saith he unto them, Render therefore unto Caesar the things that are Caesar's; and unto God the things that are God's. And when they heard it, they marvelled, and left him, and went away. (Matthew 22:15–22).

The question they asked Jesus was very difficult to answer without getting into serious trouble, because if he said no, don't pay taxes to Caesar, that money belongs to God, he would have pleased the Jews, but he would have faced serious problems with the Roman government. If he would have said yes, it is only right to pay the taxes you owe, the Jews would attack him. The answer with which Jesus responded was perfect.

The questions the Pharisees and elders had been asking Jesus allowed him to ask them a question they could not answer.

> Now while the Pharisees were gathered together, Jesus asked them a question, saying, What think ye of the Christ? whose son is he? They say unto him, The son of David. He saith unto them, How then doth David in the Spirit call him Lord, saying, The Lord said unto my Lord, Sit thou on my right hand, Till I put thine enemies underneath thy feet? If David then calleth him Lord, how is he his son? And no one was able to answer him a word, neither durst any man from that day forth ask him any more questions. (Matthew 22:41–46)

Jesus as God is the root of David. Jesus as the Son of man is the Branch of David. In any case, Jesus is the righteous Branch that Jehovah raised up to become the Son of man, the Son of David, and the Son of God; and his name is *Jehovah, our righteousness.* No one wears that holy name but the almighty "*I AM*" Jehovah God himself. Jesus is Jehovah, the "*I AM*" who called Moses to the burning bush and told him to take off his shoes, for he was standing on holy ground.

Isaiah wrote that the One who was coming to redeem the creation and become the Savior of the world would be the Almighty God himself, and his name is Jehovah. But the words Isaiah wrote were written to describe Jesus, the very one who was to become the Son of God, and they are very powerful words. Isaiah wrote,

> For unto us a child is born, unto us a son is given; and the government shall be upon his shoulder: and his name shall be called Wonderful, Counsellor, Mighty God, Everlasting Father, Prince of Peace. Of the increase of his government and of peace there shall be no end, upon the throne of David, and upon his kingdom, to establish it, and to uphold it with justice and with righteousness from henceforth even for ever. The zeal of Jehovah of hosts will perform this. (Isaiah 9:6-7)

The "us" to whom the Son was born is God; he was born of a woman, born under the Law, and God was his Father (Galatians 4:4). He was born to keep that law perfectly and then offer his flawless life to God as a sacrifice to take away the sins of the world (John 1:29). Therefore, the "us" to whom the Son was given was also God, and he gave himself to the Almighty as a sacrifice to take away the sins of the world (John 1:29) and restore the world back into its original perfection. God is One, and there is one God (Ephesians 4:4-6). However, God is three persons, or three personalities. He is the Father, the Son (the Word), and the Holy Spirit (Matthew 28:18-20; 1

Corinthians 12:4-6; 2 Corinthians 13:14). It is he who said, "*Let us make man in our image*" (plural) (Genesis 1:26-27), and he is the "*us*" to whom the Son was born, and to whom the Son was given.

The word *Jehovah* never appears in the New Testament, but the New Covenant clearly identifies Jesus as God. Jesus, who is called God in the New Testament (John 1:1-2), is the Christian's Master—just as he was called Jehovah in the Old Covenant, and he was Israel's Master. Jesus, who is the God of the New Covenant is the same One who is called Jehovah, the God of the Old Covenant, and in him lives the Father, the Son (the Word), and the Holy Spirit (Matthew 28:18-20). It is the Word of God who became the Son of God when he was born to a woman who was a virgin (John 1:1-3, 14; Galatians 4:4), and her name was Mary (Matthew 1:18-24).

After Jesus had finished his ministry, he and his eleven apostles went to the Mount from which he was about to ascend into heaven, and that is when he gave his apostles the Great Commission. Some of Jesus' apostles who went with him to the mount still doubted that the one they were with was the same real man, the Christ, who had been living with them for over three years. They could not believe anyone could be raised from the dead. Matthew wrote,

> But the eleven disciples went into Galilee, unto the mountain where Jesus had appointed them. And when they saw him, they worshipped him; but some doubted. And Jesus came to them and spake

unto them, saying, All authority hath been
given unto me in heaven and on earth. Go
ye therefore, and make disciples of all the
nations, baptizing them into the name of
the Father and of the Son and of the Holy
Spirit: teaching them to observe all things
whatsoever I commanded you: and lo, I
am with you always, even unto the end of
the world. (Matthew 28:16-20)

Matthew wrote that baptism is to be administered in
the name of the Father, the Son, and the Holy Spirit, the
three members of the Godhead, for they are the fullness
of God (Matthew 28:18-20). But the fulness of God also
dwells in Jesus. Paul wrote, "Take heed lest there shall be
any one that maketh spoil of you through his philosophy
and vain deceit, after the tradition of men, after the rudiments of the world, and not after Christ: for in him dwelleth all the fulness of the Godhead bodily" (Colossians
2:8-9). That is why Paul and Peter administered baptism
in the name of Jesus, for he is the fullness of the Godhead
(Acts 2:38; 8:16; 10:48). That is something that is very
difficult to understand, but it can be understood by just
accepting it and believing it in faith.

The New Testament letters identify Jesus as God.
John wrote,

In the beginning was the Word, and the
Word was with God, and the Word was
God. The same was in the beginning with
God. All things were made through him;
and without him was not anything made

that hath been made. In him was life; and the life was the light of men...And the Word became flesh, and dwelt among us (and we beheld his glory, glory as of the only begotten from the Father), full of grace and truth. (John 1:1-14)

John and Paul were in perfect agreement when they both declared Jesus to be the Almighty, and the Creator of all things. Paul wrote,

Who is the image of the invisible God, the firstborn of all creation; for in him were all things created, in the heavens and upon the earth, things visible and things invisible, whether thrones or dominions or principalities or powers; all things have been created through him, and unto him; and he is before all things, and in him all things consist. And he is the head of the body, the church: who is the beginning, the firstborn from the dead; that in all things he might have the preeminence. For it was the good pleasure of the Father that in him should all the fulness dwell; and through him to reconcile all things unto himself, having made peace through the blood of his cross; through him, I say, whether things upon the earth, or things in the heavens. (Colossians 1:15-20)

The Hebrew author wrote it was God who built all things. He wrote, "For he hath been counted worthy of more glory than Moses, by so much as he that built the house hath more honor than the house. For every house is builded by some one; but he that built all things is God" (Hebrews 3:3-4).

The beginning of the creation is recorded in Genesis, where Moses wrote,

> In the beginning God created the heavens and the earth. And the earth was waste and void; and darkness was upon the face of the deep: and the Spirit of God moved upon the face of the waters. And God said, Let there be light: and there was light. And God saw the light, that it was good: and God divided the light from the darkness. And God called the light Day, and the darkness he called Night. And there was evening and there was morning, one day. (Genesis 1:1-5)

The above scripture is an account of how the world and the universe in which we live came into its existence. It was the Father who designed the entire creation in his mind, from the planet earth to the farthest star. Then he spoke what he had designed. The Psalmist wrote,

> Praise ye him, sun and moon: Praise him, all ye stars of light. Praise him, ye heavens of heavens, and ye waters that are above the heavens. Let them praise the name

of Jehovah; For he commanded, and they were created. (Psalms 148:3-5)

By the word of Jehovah were the heavens made, And all the host of them by the breath of his mouth. He gathereth the waters of the sea together as a heap: He layeth up the deeps in store-houses. Let all the earth fear Jehovah: Let all the inhabitants of the world stand in awe of him. For he spake, and it was done; He commanded, and it stood fast. (Psalms 33:6-9)

When God created the stars, he counted them and called them by their names. The Psalmist wrote, "He counteth the number of the stars; He calleth them all by their names. Great is our Lord, and mighty in power; His understanding is infinite" (Palms 147:4-5).

It is encouraging to know that if the mind of God is so infinite that he can count and name all the stars, and remember them and their names, he certainly can remember all his children, their works, and their names.

It was the Word who grasped what the Father had designed and spoken, and He fashioned it into a real, actual, physical creation. But what the Word created was waste, void, and dark. It was nothing but space, a place to put things (it is exceedingly difficult to understand how space could have been created, what was here before it was created?), mass (or matter), the ninety-four basic elements from which all things are made and occupy space, energy (light), which is the power necessary to make the world function, and time, a way to measure and control all the events that take place in the world. Then it was the Spirit who moved, or vibrated over what the Word created, and he organized it into the perfectly ordered and predictable world we live in today. It was the Spirit who created the laws of the universe, or the laws nature and physics, such as the law of gravity, the law of thermodynamics, the laws of motion; and these are the natural laws of God man cannot break.

The New Testament defines who Jesus is, that he truly is God, the great *"I AM."* Paul wrote of Jesus as being our Savior and our great God, and the very one who came into the world to save his children from sin and death. Paul wrote,

> For the grace of God hath appeared, bringing salvation to all men, instructing us, to the intent that, denying ungodliness and worldly lusts, we should live soberly and righteously and godly in this present world; looking for the blessed hope and appearing of the glory of the great God and our Saviour Jesus Christ; who gave himself for us, that he might redeem us from all iniquity, and purify unto himself a people for his own possession, zealous of good works. (Titus 2:11-15)

The Hebrew author wrote of the occasion when God, the Father, addressed his Son, the Word, by calling him *"God,"* and he also addressed him as *"Lord."* He wrote,

And when he again bringeth in the first-born into the world he saith, And let all the angels of God worship him. And of the angels he saith, Who maketh his angels winds, and his ministers a flame of fire: but of the Son he saith, Thy throne, O God, is forever and ever; and the sceptre of uprightness is the sceptre of thy kingdom. Thou hast loved righteousness, and hated iniquity; therefore God, thy God, hath anointed thee With the oil of gladness above thy fellows. And, Thou, Lord, in the beginning didst lay the foundation of the earth, And the heavens are the works of thy hands: (Hebrews 1:6-10)

It is written here that God called Jesus, his Son, *God*, and *Lord*, and he told him that he sat on an eternal throne, which means he is forever the Master over everything. God commanded the angels to worship his Son as the Almighty *"I AM"* because that is who he is. Angels are not to be worshiped (Colossians 2:18) for they are fellow-servants of the Most High God, as such also are the Christians (Revelation 22:8-9). But the angels were commanded to worship Jesus, as were the apostles and all men so commanded.

There was a time after Jesus had been raised from the dead that he met with his apostles, but Thomas was not among them (John 20:19–24). On that occasion the ten apostles who had seen Jesus told Thomas they had seen the risen Lord and he was well and alive. Thomas refused to believe them. Jesus, knowing all things, arranged the meeting that was necessary to convince his *doubting apostle* that he had been raised from the dead, and that he was indeed well and alive. John wrote,

> The other disciples therefore said unto him, We have seen the Lord. But he said unto them, Except I shall see in his hands the print of the nails, and put my hand into his side, I will not believe. And after eight days again his disciples were within, and Thomas with them. Jesus cometh, the doors being shut, and stood in the midst, and said, Peace be unto you. Then saith he to Thomas, Reach hither thy finger, and see my hands; and reach hither thy hand, and put it into my side: and be not faithless, but believing. Thomas answered and said unto him, My Lord and my God. Jesus saith unto him, Because thou hast seen me, thou hast believed: blessed are they that have not seen, and yet have believed. (John 20:25–29)

Thomas fell before Jesus and worshipped him, and he called Jesus his Lord and his God. Jesus accepted his praise. Had that not been a true statement it would never have been allowed by the Father, nor would Jesus have accepted being worshipped as God. But Jesus accepted glory, praise, and worship from this man because he is God. On another occasion there was a man who was not God, but who accepted the praise from men that belongs only to God—and that man was immediately eaten by worms—and he died; his name was Herod (Acts 12:21–24).

Jesus made a statement about himself receiving glory from men, and his words are greatly misunderstood when they are not viewed in the context in which they were spoken. Jesus said, "*I receive not glory from men*" (John 5:41). That statement cannot mean Jesus does not accept glory from men, or that he refuses to be praised and worshiped by men. Thomas had just fallen to his knees and praised and worshipped Jesus, and Jesus accepted his praise and glory. Also, the reason we go to church is to worship God and to praise and glorify his Son, Jesus—just as Thomas did. We sing songs of praise to Jesus because he is our Savior, songs like, "*Praise him, praise him, Jesus our blessed Redeemer.*" Therefore, if we view Jesus' statement in the context in which it was written, we shall see clearly that Jesus not only receives praise and glory from men, but he earnestly desires it.

If we worship and glorify the Father, we can only do so by first worshipping and glorifying Jesus, his Son. John wrote, "For neither doth the Father judge any man, but he hath given all judgment unto the Son; that all may honor the Son, even as they honor the Father. He that honoreth not the Son honoreth not the Father that sent him" (John 5:22-23). In that same context, just a few words below, Jesus said, "I receive not glory from men" (John 5:41). Why would John say the only way to worship God was through Jesus, and Jesus himself say the only way to praise God and honor the Father was through him (John 14:6), and then Jesus say he would not accept that praise and glory? That just does not make sense. The next thing we should view is the reason Jesus said, "*I receive not glory from men.*" John continued writing,

> And the Father that sent me, he hath borne witness of me. Ye have neither heard his voice at any time, nor seen his form. And ye have not his word abiding in you: for whom he sent, him ye believe not. Ye search the scriptures, because ye think that in them ye have eternal life; and these are they which bear witness of me; and ye will not come to me, that ye may have life. I receive not glory from men. (John 5:37–41)

When we read that scripture in its context, *we see five reasons* that make it very clear why Jesus did not receive glory from men. It was not because he refused to be glorified by men, and therefore he would not accept their praise and worship; it was: *(1)* because men did not accept the witness the Father had borne concerning His Son, whom he had sent; *(2)* they did not believe Jesus was the Christ who had been sent by the Father; *(3)* they did not have God's Word abiding in them; *(4)* they did not come to the One whom God had sent and accept him as their Lord and Savior; *(5)* and they did not believe the scriptures they searched daily that said he was coming. Those are the reasons Jesus said he did not receive praise and glory from men—*there was no glory and praise for Jesus to receive!*

There was never an occasion, and there were many of them, when someone bowed before Jesus and worshipped him, including Doubting Thomas (John 20:24–29), that Jesus refused to accept their praise (Matthew 8:1-3; 14:26-33; 15:22-25; 28:9-10, 16-17). Only God is worthy of our praise, glory, and worship, and Jesus is God.

Peter, Jesus' apostle, knew who Jesus was not long after they met. There was an occasion when Peter and his crew had been fishing all night and caught nothing. Then Jesus stepped into his boat and told him to try it again, in the deep. Peter, reluctantly, obeyed Jesus, and he caught so many fish his nets were starting to come apart. That is the moment when Peter realized who Jesus was, the Almighty, and he fell to his knees and worshiped him. Luke wrote, "But Simon Peter, when he saw it, fell down at Jesus' knees, saying, Depart from me; for I am a sinful man, O Lord" (Luke 5:8). Peter wrote in his second epistle, "Simon Peter, a servant and apostle of Jesus Christ, to them that have obtained a like precious faith with us in the righteousness of our God and the Saviour Jesus Christ" (2 Peter 1:1)

The apostle John also knew who Jesus was (John 1:1-3, 14). He knew Jesus was the true God and eternal life. He wrote,

> We know that we are of God, and the whole world lieth in the evil one. And we know that the Son of God is come, and hath given us an understanding, that we know him that is true, and we are in him

that is true, even in his Son Jesus Christ.
This is the true God, and eternal life. My
little children, guard yourselves from
idols. (1 John 5:19-21)

Even the demons knew who Jesus was, for they must
have had known him as the Almighty, the *"I AM,"* before
the foundation of the world, and before he became the
Son of God, and the Son of Man.

Jesus met two men who were possessed with many
demons, and they wanted to be cleansed from their infir-
mity. Jesus healed the men and cast out the demons. The
demons not only knew who Jesus was, the Christ, but
they knew he reigned supreme, and he would be their
judge—and they even knew when that judgment was going to occur. Matthew wrote,

And when he was come to the other side
into the country of the Gadarenes, there
met him two possessed with demons,
coming forth out of the tombs, exceeding
fierce, so that no man could pass by that
way. And behold, they cried out, saying,
What have we to do with thee, thou Son
of God? art thou come hither to torment
us before the time? (Matthew 8:28-29).

Luke wrote of several occasions when Jesus cleansed
men from being demon possessed.

And in the synagogue there was a man,
that had a spirit of an unclean demon;

and he cried out with a loud voice, Ah!
what have we to do with thee, Jesus thou
Nazarene? art thou come to destroy us? I
know thee who thou art, the Holy One of
God. And Jesus rebuked him, saying, Hold
thy peace, and come out of him. And when
the demon had thrown him down in the
midst, he came out of him, having done
him no hurt. And amazement came upon
all, and they spake together, one with another, saying, What is this word? for with
authority and power he commandeth the
unclean spirits, and they come out. (Luke
4:33-36)

And when the sun was setting, all they that
had any sick with divers diseases brought
them unto him; and he laid his hands on
every one of them, and healed them. And
demons also came out from many, crying
out, and saying, Thou art the Son of God.
And rebuking them, he suffered them not
to speak, because they knew that he was
the Christ. (Luke 4:40-41)

Jesus did not want demons testifying for him, and neither did Paul, the apostle. Luke wrote,

And it came to pass, as we were going to the place of prayer, that a certain
maid having a spirit of divination met
us, who brought her masters much gain

by soothsaying. The same following after Paul and us cried out, saying, These men are servants of the Most High God, who proclaim unto you the way of salvation. And this she did for many days. But Paul, being sore troubled, turned and said to the spirit, I charge thee in the name of Jesus Christ to come out of her. And it came out that very hour. (Acts 16:16-18)

The maid who was proclaiming Paul to be a servant of the Most High God, and that he was teaching the way of salvation was declaring the truth. But Paul did not want someone who was possessed by Satan to be the one announcing him in such fashion.

Is it possible for people to be demon possessed today? Paul wrote,

And the Lord's servant must not strive, but be gentle towards all, apt to teach, forbearing, in meekness correcting them that oppose themselves; if peradventure God may give them repentance unto the knowledge of the truth, and they may recover themselves out of the snare of the devil, having been taken captive by him unto his will. (2 Timothy 2:24-26)

Being demon possessed today might not be exactly as it was during the time of Christ, but according to the words of Paul—*it can happen.* When men behave themselves in such evil ways that they become obnoxious—and they even make laws that are absolutely contrary to the Word of God, such as the laws allowing abortion, and laws that are against the proper, scriptural marriage relationships—they are teaching the ways of Satan and giving place the ways the devil loves. There is also a way out of it, and that is by a person realizing what has happened to them, and recovering from it by trusting and obeying God, and in the name of Jesus demanding the evil spirits depart, and leave them alone, all in the powerful name of Jesus.

CHAPTER 2

✳

"*I AM*" JESUS — THE SON OF MAN

WHEN GOD CREATED THE world in which we live he knew before the first day of the creation that sin would enter his world and defile it. He knew something would have to be done to redeem it, or otherwise it must be judged and destroyed according to the law he had given Adam when he placed him in the garden. Therefore, God knew before he created the world the cross would be necessary to redeem it. Peter wrote,

> And if ye call on him as Father, who without respect of persons judgeth according to each man's work, pass the time of your sojourning in fear: knowing that ye were

redeemed, not with corruptible things, with silver or gold, from your vain manner of life handed down from your fathers; but with precious blood, as of a lamb without spot, even the blood of Christ: who was foreknown indeed before the foundation of the world, but was manifested at the end of the times for your sake, who through him are believers in God, that raised him from the dead, and gave him glory; so that your faith and hope might be in God. (1 Peter 1:17-21)

The plan God established in his mind before he created the world was not to destroy the creation and the entire human family with it by enforcing the death penalty he had pronounced against sin, and implementing the condemnation he had decreed against Adam and Eve for breaking the one simple commandment he had given them—"*stay away from my tree!*"—but God's plan was to forgive them, *and all sinners*, and restore everything back into its original perfection, or better. He would accomplish his purpose by the blood of the cross of his own Son. God would become a man, and that man would take all the sins, and all the punishment and condemnation for sin upon himself, and he would suffer the death all sinners deserved, and pay in full for all sin once and for all by his own death. For God to achieve his objective he must leave his throne of glory in heaven and become a man, and he must live on the earth as a man—a man exactly like all other men. He must experience all the

dangers, threats, frailties, limitations, and physical infir-
mities that other men face with no advantages over them
whatsoever. At the end of his life his plan was to offer
himself and his perfect life to God as a human sacrifice to
take away the sins of the world (John 1:29), to pay for all
the damage sin had caused, and correct all the problems
that sin had produced.

Paul wrote that the coming of Jesus would happen according to God's eternal purpose; an eternal purpose has
no beginning, and it has no end. Paul wrote,

> And to make all men see what is the dispen-
> sation of the mystery which for ages hath
> been hid in God who created all things; to
> the intent that now unto the principali-
> ties and the powers in the heavenly places
> might be made known through the church
> the manifold wisdom of God, according to
> the eternal purpose which he purposed in
> Christ Jesus our Lord. (Ephesians 3:9–11)

It was a very serious matter that required God to
leave his Holy Place in heaven and become a man. When
God lived in his Holy Place in heaven he had all power,
all authority, and all knowledge, and his holiness was
constantly protected by his mighty angels and his inap-
proachable light (1 Timothy 6:13–16). No one, not even
an angel could approach him in his Holy Place unless
they had been invited. Even so, the *I AM* left his Holy
Place to become a man. That required him to give up his
equality with God and become a man in all points just
like all other men. Paul wrote,

Have this mind in you, which was also in
Christ Jesus: who, existing in the form of
God, counted not the being on an equality
with God a thing to be grasped, but emptied himself, taking the form of a servant,
being made in the likeness of men; and
being found in fashion as a man, he hum-
bled himself, becoming obedient even
unto death, yea, the death of the cross.
(Philippians 2:5-8)

When Jesus emptied himself of his equality with God,
he had none of attributes of God left in him whatsoever;
he became a man in all points exactly like all other men.
The Hebrew author wrote,

Wherefore it behooved him in all things
to be made like unto his brethren, that he
might become a merciful and faithful high
priest in things pertaining to God, to make
propitiation for the sins of the people. For
in that he himself hath suffered being
tempted, he is able to succor them that are
tempted. (Hebrews 2:17-18)

Putting this all together it means that when Jesus
came into the world to redeem his creation and restore
all things back into their original perfection (Acts 3:21)
he gave up his equality with God and he became a man
just exactly like all other men to accomplish that—with
one exception—he was still the Almighty Jehovah "*I AM*"
living in his body. Paul wrote, "Take heed lest there shall

be any one that maketh spoil of you through his philosophy and vain deceit, after the tradition of men, after the
rudiments of the world, and not after Christ: for in him
dwelleth all the fulness of the Godhead bodily, and in
him ye are made full, who is the head of all principality
and power" (Colossians 2:8-10).

Jesus grew up like all other children grow and learn;
he was taught well by his parents, and by his heavenly
Father also. Luke wrote in his gospel, "And the child grew,
and waxed strong, filled with wisdom: and the grace of
God was upon him...And Jesus advanced in wisdom and
stature, and in favor with God and men" (Luke 2:40, 52).

Jesus grew up with brothers and sisters in a very poor
family. He knew the problems that family relationships
face.

> And coming into his own country he
> taught them in their synagogue, inso-
> much that they were astonished, and said,
> Whence hath this man this wisdom, and
> these mighty works? Is not this the car-
> penter's son? is not his mother called
> Mary? and his brethren, James, and Joseph,
> and Simon, and Judas? And his sisters, are
> they not all with us? Whence then hath
> this man all these things? And they were
> offended in him. (Matthew 13:54–57)

It is quite unreasonable for anyone to be jealous of
another person, and to be offended in them just because they are highly intelligent and capable of doing
great things. But even Jesus' brothers and sisters did

not believe in him, and even they were offended in him (John 7:1–5).

Jesus, throughout his entire life, lived just like all other men must live, and he had no advantages over them whatsoever. After he left his home with Joseph and Mary, he did not even have a place to sleep. Matthew wrote, "And there came a scribe, and said unto him, Teacher, I will follow thee whithersoever thou goest. And Jesus saith unto him, The foxes have holes, and the birds of the heaven have nests; but the Son of man hath not where to lay his head" (Matthew 8:19–20). There was no response from the scribe. Jesus lived like a street person—a person with no real home. But Jesus' real home was not in this world—his real home was a kingdom, and he was the King, and it is called the kingdom of heaven, or the kingdom of God.

Jesus had no more power *within himself* to accomplish anything above what any other man could do. No man had the power to work miracles unless that power had been given to them by the great "I AM." When Jesus performed miracles, such as healing the sick, giving sight to the blind, and raising the dead, he did not do so by his own power; he did it by calling upon his Father for that ability (John 11:40-43). Jesus never worked a miracle, nor did he escape the temptations, the difficulties, and the troubles of life by calling upon his own divine power to do so; and he had that power within him because he was God—Jesus had to rely on his Father to provide for his needs, his protection, and his security—just exactly as all other men must trust God for all things, and it was he, who put himself into that position.

Had Jesus chosen to use his own divine power as God to conquer the problems he faced, and to overcome sin, death, and even escape Hades, he would have been different than other men. He would have had a tremendous advantage over other men, and therefore he could not have become their High Priest (Hebrews 4:15; 5:1–4), because other men have no such powers. Only as a man like all other men could Jesus have become the Lamb of God to offer himself as the perfect human sacrifice to take away the sins of the world (John 1:29), abolish death (2 Timothy 1:10), and become our High Priest (Hebrews 5:1-4).

If Jesus would have had to call upon his own divine powers as God to overcome temptation it would have been a confession that it is not possible for just an ordinary man to live without sin, but that it takes a divine person, or divine intervention to achieve that. It would also have put men into the position of being commanded to do something it was not possible to do—that is, to keep the law perfectly and never sin. But Jesus proved it could be accomplished by a man because he was the man who did it. Are there others who have lived without sin? Possibly so, for Enoch, the seventh from Adam never died, and death was the punishment for sin. But Enoch was taken out of this world by God when he was only 365 years of age, and he was taken *because he walked with God* (Genesis 5:21-24). Elijah was another man who never faced death, for he was taken from this earth in a fiery chariot (2 Kings 2:11). Luke wrote that the parents of John the Baptist had never sinned (Luke 1:5-6).

There was an occasion when Jesus and Peter were going into the temple. There was a temple tax, which was hardly anything at all, about a penny; but it was more than Jesus and Peter had between them. Matthew wrote of that incident.

> And when they were come to Capernaum, they that received the half-shekel came to Peter, and said, Doth not your teacher pay the half-shekel? He saith, Yea. And when he came into the house, Jesus spoke first to him, saying, What thinkest thou, Simon? the kings of the earth, from whom do they receive toll or tribute? from their sons, or from strangers? And when he said, From strangers, Jesus said unto him, Therefore the sons are free. But, lest we cause them to stumble, go thou to the sea, and cast a hook, and take up the fish that first cometh up; and when thou hast opened his mouth, thou shalt find a shekel: that take, and give unto them for me and thee. (Matthew 17:24–27)

Jesus never worried about money. He never had a dime or a peso in his pocket, if he had a pocket, and he never owned anything throughout his entire life but the clothes he wore. The soldiers who crucified him took those (Psalms 22:18; Matthew 27:35).

When Jesus entered his ministry he had many children—his children were those who believed him to be the Son of God, they were his family, and he called his children, his brethren. There is a difference in being a child who is responsible to his father, and being brothers who are equal. The Hebrew author wrote,

> For both he that sanctifies and they that are sanctified are all of one: for which cause he is not ashamed to call them brethren, saying, I will declare thy name unto my brethren, In the midst of the congregation will I sing thy praise. And again, I will put my trust in him. And again, Behold, I and the children whom God hath given me. (Hebrews 2:11–13)

The one who died to sanctify us, and we who are sanctified in him, *are all one—we are all brethren*, and *we are all one family*—we are the family of God! It is exciting to know that when we are in the church assembly with our family, and we sing praises to God, Jesus is right there with us, and he is singing with us (Matthew 18:20); and when we partake of the Communion, he is with us, and he is partaking of the Communion with us (Matthew 26:26–29). We cannot see him, but we know he is there. And again, just as our only strength is to trust God for our lives, our protection, and everything we need, so also Jesus said he would put his trust in the Father in the same manner (Hebrews 2:13). That is the way Jesus lived his entire life; he lived day by day trusting his Father for all things, which is the same way all other men must live.

We should be greatly encouraged by these words, for we have the same power living and working in us (John 14:12; Ephesians 3:20–21; Philippians 4:13), and the same blessings and promises residing in us and protecting us that lived and worked in Jesus, God's only begotten Son. The Hebrew author wrote, "Be ye free from the love of money; content with such things as ye have: for himself hath said, I will in no wise fail thee, neither will I in any wise forsake thee. So that with good courage we say, The Lord is my helper; I will not fear: What shall man do unto me?" (Hebrews 13:5-6).

Jesus lived his entire life having never sinned, not even once (John 8:46; 2 Corinthians 5:21; Hebrews 4:15). The reason Jesus never sinned is not because he was God and could not sin, but because in every decision and act he performed, and in every word he spoke, he chose not to sin. Therefore, when we are tempted so severely, and we do not think we can endure it any longer, but we keep on keeping on anyway, Jesus knows exactly how we feel and how badly temptation hurts, even when the temptation becomes so strong it seems impossible to endure it any longer. Paul wrote, "but as it is written, Things which eye saw not, and ear heard not, and which entered not into the heart of man, whatsoever things God prepared for them that love him" (1 Corinthians 2:9). The spiritual world, or the kingdom of God that He has promised to give his children is so great, so magnificent, so beautiful, and so majestic that it cannot be seen nor understood by people living in this present physical world. That is the way Jesus felt when he was in the garden praying to his Father to relieve him from having to endure the cross. Mark wrote,

And they come unto a place which was named Gethsemane: and he saith unto his disciples, Sit ye here, while I pray. And he taketh with him Peter and James and John, and began to be greatly amazed, and sore troubled. And he saith unto them, My soul is exceeding sorrowful even unto death: abide ye here, and watch. And he went forward a little, and fell on the ground, and prayed that, if it were possible, the hour might pass away from him. And he said, Abba, Father, all things are possible unto thee; remove this cup from me: howbeit not what I will, but what thou wilt. (Mark 4:32-36).

For Jesus to qualify to become our High Priest and our sacrifice, our sin-offering, and to pay in full for all the condemnation and damage sin had caused, he had to keep God's law perfectly, and he must do it as a man, not as God. Jesus could not transgress the law, not even in one point, and still be our Savior, our Sacrifice, and our High Priest. He conquered that challenge, and he lived his entire life without sin (John 8:46; 2 Corinthians 5:21; Hebrews 4:15). At the end of his life he was required to endure the cross to the end, and die, to become the perfect sacrifice that would take away the sins of the world. Then he must trust his Father for his resurrection so he could live again to become our High Priest, for the High Priest alone could present his sacrifice to God, the only sacrifice that truly would take away all the sins of the world.

When we consider what Jesus accomplished when he died on the cross, and was resurrected, we should consider the infinite power the cross has—the cross has the power to perfectly annul the transgression Adam committed, and all of its consequences; it has the power to restore all things back into their original perfection and glory, to forgive all men of the sins they have committed, and to repair all things from the damage sin had caused—and restore the creation back into its original perfection and magnificence just as it was when God created it. The cross has all the power necessary to undue all the damage and devastation sin has caused.

The coming of Jesus changed the lives of many people. Mary and Joseph would never be the same after they had raised Jesus and watched him grow up and become the Messiah. There were others; there were fishermen, tax collectors, working and professional men whose lives were changed significantly when they were called to leave their occupations and become the apostles of God. Probably the man who made the greatest change was Paul, the great Pharisee and super Israelite who gave up his life as a chief Pharisee in the Law of Moses to become a Christian, and an apostle of Jesus. It took Paul three years of desert life and isolation in Arabia to think about what had happened to him, and to overcome the shock he experienced when he learned he had been serving the wrong master (Galatians 1:13-20).

It required Jesus himself to appear to Paul in glory, as the Almighty "*I AM*," to convince him he must make that change, to stop persecuting Christians, and become a Christian himself. God knew what he was requiring of Paul, and of all the men whom he had called to leave their occupations and serve him, and he did not tell them it would be easy, but he did tell them it would be worth it.

After Jesus finished his ministry and he was on the holy mount with his disciples, and he was about to ascend back into heaven, he said,

> All authority hath been given unto me in heaven and on earth. Go ye therefore, and make disciples of all the nations, baptizing them into the name of the Father and of the Son and of the Holy Spirit: teaching them to observe all things whatsoever I commanded you: and lo, I am with you always, even unto the end of the world. (Matthew 28:18-20)

It was by Jesus' death on the cross and his resurrection that he was given all authority to establish his kingdom on earth, and his kingdom is a perfect, holy, and righteous spiritual kingdom. It is called the church, the kingdom of God, and the kingdom of heaven, and it was created to live and function in this present evil world, and in all the cultures of all the different nations of the world, but it would never be part of the world (2 Corinthians 6:12-18; Galatians 1:4).

Before Jesus became the Son of man he had all the authority of God, because he is God. He gave up that authority when he became the Son of man and he emptied himself of his equality with God. When Jesus finished his work on earth and was ready to ascend back into heaven, his Father gave him back the authority he had before he became the Son of man; but it was delegated authority he received from his Father as the Son of man, and not the authority he had in himself as the great "*I AM*." That was the reward God gave him for what he had accomplished; Jesus had saved the entire creation and all of God's children from death and annihilation.

Jesus realized the limitations he placed upon himself by the position he took as a man when he voluntarily gave his equality with God. John wrote,

> Jesus therefore answered and said unto them, Verily, verily, I say unto you, The Son can do nothing of himself, but what he seeth the Father doing: for what things so ever he doeth, these the Son also doeth in like manner. (John 5:19)

I can of myself do nothing: as I hear, I judge: and my judgment is righteous; because I seek not mine own will, but the will of him that sent me. (John 5:30)

> Jesus therefore said, When ye have lifted up the Son of man, then shall ye know that I am he, and that I do nothing of myself, but as the Father taught me, I speak these things. And he that sent me is with me; he hath not left me alone; for I do always the things that are pleasing to him. As he spoke these things, many believed on him. (John 8:28–29)

CHAPTER 3

"I AM" JESUS — THE WAY, THE TRUTH, THE LIFE, THE RESURRECTION

GOD'S NATION, ISRAEL, LATER to become the kingdom of God, started as a small group of about seventy-five souls (Acts 7:14). The Israelites were the descendants of the son of Terah, and Terah's son was called Abram, and it was through him that God promised the Israelites He would be with them and He would make them into a great nation. The nation of Israel was promised security, good health, good crops, many children, many cattle, and great wealth, and it was the great "*I AM*," Jehovah, who had delivered them from Egyptian slavery who promised Israel all those blessings, and it was Jehovah who ruled Israel as his covenant God, his Master, his Teacher, his Provider, his Comforter, and his Savior—*but there was a condition*: they were required to obey God and keep his commandments.

> Now Jehovah said unto Abram, Get thee out of thy country, and from thy kindred, and from thy father's house, unto the land that I will show thee: and I will make of thee a great nation, and I will bless thee, and make thy name great; and be thou a blessing: and I will bless them that bless thee, and him that curseth thee will I curse: and in thee shall all the families of the earth be blessed. (Genesis 12:1-3)

> And Jehovah said unto Abram, after that Lot was separated from him, Lift up now thine eyes, and look from the place where thou art, northward and southward and eastward and westward: for all the land which thou seest, to thee will I give it, and to thy seed for ever. And I will make thy seed as the dust of the earth: so that if a man can number the dust of the earth, then may thy seed also be numbered. Arise, walk through the land in the length of it and in the breadth of it; for unto thee will I give it. And Abram moved his tent,

and came and dwelt by the oaks of Mamre,
which are in Hebron, and built there an altar unto Jehovah. (Genesis 13:14-18)

Abram was seventy-five when he was called to leave
Haran, Sarah was sixty-five, and Abram and Sarah had
been married for some time, but they had no children,
and God had promised Abram he would become a great
nation—and that requires many, many children. Abram
believed God and he and Sarah packed up and moved.
Abram and Sarah went to the gate of the city, and he
asked God, "Which way, Lord?" God said, "Start walk-
ing." Abraham obeyed God and he and Sarah went as
God commanded them, and many years later Abram and
Sarah still had no children, and he was concerned. Moses
wrote,

After these things the word of Jehovah
came unto Abram in a vision, saying, Fear
not, Abram: I am thy shield, and thy exceeding great reward. And Abram said,
O Lord Jehovah, what wilt thou give me,
seeing I go childless, and he that shall
be possessor of my house is Eliezer of
Damascus? And Abram said, Behold, to
me thou hast given no seed: and, lo, one
born in my house is mine heir.

And, behold, the word of Jehovah came
unto him, saying, This man shall not be
thine heir; but he that shall come forth
out of thine own bowels shall be thine

> heir. And he brought him forth abroad,
> and said, Look now toward heaven, and
> number the stars, if thou be able to num-
> ber them: and he said unto him, So shall
> thy seed be. And he believed in Jehovah;
> and he reckoned it to him for righteous-
> ness. (Genesis 15:1-6)

It was some twenty-five years later that God again appeared to Abram and promised him a son. Abram was
ninety-nine years of age and Sarah was ninety (Genesis
17:1, 17), and by that time Abram had given up on
God's promise—he did not see how it could be fulfilled
(Genesis 17:17-18) —and every day made such an event
seem even more and more impossible. Abram's response
to God was, "Then Abram fell upon his face, and laughed,
and said in his heart, Shall a child be born unto him that
is a hundred years old? and shall Sarah, that is ninety
years old, bear?" (Genesis 17:17). Sarah had the same
response,

> And God said, I will certainly return unto
> thee when the season cometh round; and,
> lo, Sarah thy wife shall have a son. And
> Sarah heard in the tent door, which was
> behind him. Now Abraham and Sarah
> were old, and well stricken in age; it had
> ceased to be with Sarah after the man-
> ner of women. And Sarah laughed with-
> in herself, saying, After I am waxed old
> shall I have pleasure, my lord being old
> also? (Genesis 18:10-12)

But again, Abram believed God and again it was reckoned to him for righteousness (Genesis 15:6), and it was at that time Abram's name was changed from Abram (exalted father) to Abraham (the father of a multitude) (Genesis 17:5).

It should be so very encouraging for Christian's today to see that Abraham's faith was not perfect, and when things did not transpire as Abraham thought they should, he had serious doubts they ever would happen. That means the doubts and skepticisms Christians experience in this present age shall not be held against them if they, like Abraham, just keep on keeping on living by faith and working for God. Isaiah wrote, "but they that wait for Jehovah shall renew their strength; they shall mount up with wings as eagles; they shall run, and not be weary; they shall walk, and not faint" (Isaiah 40:31).

When Christians believe Jesus' promises, they also are reckoned righteous by their faith, but they are not called friends of God, *they are called sons of God* (Luke 20:36; 1 John 3:2), for they are the family of God, and a son is greater than a friend (Hebrews 3:5-6).

Abraham had the son God promised him, and he was called Isaac (laughter) because of all the laughter Sarah experienced when she doubted she would ever have that son (Genesis 18:12; 21:6-7).

Isaac became the father of Jacob and Esau, and Jacob became the father of the twelve patriarchs who became the twelve tribes of Israel (Acts 7:8). Those twelve patriarchs, or the fathers of the twelve tribes of Israel were given the land of Canaan for their homeland, just as God promised them (Exodus 6:1-4). It was during that time

Jacob's twelve children grew to become the seventy-five souls that left their homeland because of a severe famine, and they went to Egypt for food (Acts 7:14). It was those seventy-five children of Jacob that went into Egyptian bondage for 430 years, and during that time they became the mighty nation of Israel, the nation that Pharoah feared, and the great nation God created to become his kingdom; the kingdom of heaven.

The kingdom of Israel was called *Israel* because it was named after Jacob, the son of Isaac, the son of Abraham, whose name was changed from Jacob (Supplanter, Genesis 27:36) to Israel (He who has striven with God, and prevailed, Genesis 32:28; 35:10). During Israel's captivity that nation became so great, and so powerful, that Pharoah feared the Israelites would rebel and either walk out of Egypt or take over the land. Moses wrote,

> Now there arose a new king over Egypt, who knew not Joseph. And he said unto his people, Behold, the people of the children of Israel are more and mightier than we: come, let us deal wisely with them, lest they multiply, and it come to pass, that, when there falleth out any war, they also join themselves unto our enemies, and fight against us, and get them up out of the land. (Exodus 1:8-10).

It was during that time Moses was called to the burning bush and God commanded him to go back to Egypt and deliver his children from their bondage. He did.

When the Israelites were liberated from slavery they became the nation of Israel, and later they became the kingdom of God, and Jehovah was their Master and their King (1 Samuel 8:4-9). He ruled Israel with great love. He was Israel's covenant God, and he gave Israel the Law of Moses and the priesthood of Levi. Israel was God's chosen nation, for Israel alone was his pride and joy. The Psalmist wrote, "He showeth his word unto Jacob, His statutes and his ordinances unto Israel. He hath not dealt so with any nation; And as for his ordinances, they have not known them. Praise ye Jehovah" (Psalms 147:19-20).

When Jesus was born to Mary to become the Messiah (Matthew 1:20-21) he ruled *the Israel of God* (Galatians 6:16), the church, with the same love, passion, and power with which Jehovah had ruled the Israelites under the Law of Moses, and he ruled by his love, not by law. He was to be called Jesus and he became many things to all people; his promises were made to all people of all nations, and not just to the house of Israel. Therefore, Just as God had blessed his chosen nation Israel with a wonderful life and great security, so also Christ has blessed his children in the church, and their blessings shall be even much greater. The blessings God promised to Israel were physical blessings in a physical land, and they all passed away with time; the blessings Christians are promised are spiritual blessings in a spiritual kingdom, and they are eternal, and it is the saints who own that kingdom (Luke 12:31-32). But before any person can benefit from Jesus' promises they are required to believe in him (Hebrews 11:6) and keep his commandments (John 14:15; 1 John 2:1-6).

Written below are the blessings all men can experience, and not just Israel, if they will believe in Jesus as the Son of God, the great "*I AM*," and keep his commandments. Jesus said, "Come unto me, all ye that labor and are heavy laden, and I will give you rest. Take my yoke upon you, and learn of me; for I am meek and lowly in heart: and ye shall find rest unto your souls. For my yoke is easy, and my burden is light" (Matthew 11:28-30). The *rest* Jesus promised was not just for Israel, *it is for all men of all time,* if they will accept entering Jesus' rest under his conditions. Jesus said, Come unto me *all ye that labor*, not all ye that labor in the house of Israel. Rest for the body can be accomplished by sleep and relaxation, but rest for the soul can be attained only in Jesus.

Jesus said he was meek, or humble, and the burden he requires us to bear is light. Under the New Covenant Jesus is quite approachable by all men of all nations, and anyone can come to him for any reason at any time. Jesus wants all men to come to him with their problems because he is the solution to all our struggles, if we will just seek it.

It is difficult to see Jehovah, under the Old Covenant, as being meek and humble, and the burden the Israelites were required to carry–*keeping the Law of Moses*–as being light. When the world turned sour and sin was as bad as it could be, God destroyed it with a universal flood (Genesis 6:5-7), and all land-living creatures died except for those who were on the ark with Noah. However, through Noah, a preacher of righteousness (2 Peter 2:5), God gave the evil men living in the world 120 years advance notice of what was going to happen–if they did not repent and leave their evil ways (Genesis 6:3). They didn't. When Sodom and Gomorrah became so immoral and corrupt that they could no longer be tolerated, God destroyed all five of their cities with fire (Genesis 19:23-29). On the day the tabernacle had been completed and Israel was dedicating it to God, Nadab and Abihu, who were priests, and the sons of Aaron, the High Priest, attempted to approach God in his Most Holy Place. They were drawing near to God without having been commanded to do so. They were burned to ashes in their priestly robes in just one moment, but their clothes were not touched by the fire (Leviticus 10:1-5). They probably had been drinking a little wine or strong drink (Leviticus 10:8-10). God is love (1 John 4:8, 16), but God is also a consuming fire (Hebrews 12:29). Under the Old Covenant no one could approach the Almighty unless they had been commanded to do so. Under the New Covenant all mankind are invited to approach Jesus and come to him in faith at anytime and anywhere and for any reason. What a difference the cross made.

Under the New Covenant we serve a Master who has walked in our shoes, and who has been tempted in all points as we are tempted (Hebrews 4:15), and he personally knows the terrible force of temptation, and the pain and the struggles men have in trying to live for God and not sin (Hebrews 2:18). The Hebrew author wrote,

> For every high priest, being taken from among men, is appointed for men in things pertaining to God, that he may offer both gifts and sacrifices for sins: who can bear

gently with the ignorant and erring, for
that he himself also is compassed with in-
firmity; and by reason thereof is bound, as
for the people, so also for himself, to offer
for sins. (Hebrews 5:1-3)

Jesus is our High Priest (Hebrews 4:14-15), and according to the requirement of the law he was taken
from among men to fill that position (Hebrews 5:1-5).
All priests had to be taken from among men so they
could personally know firsthand, by experience, the difficulties, the struggles, and the problems men face in
just trying to live day by day in a very difficult and severe world—and resist temptation by not sinning. That
knowledge was necessary so the priests could deal with
men who had sinned in a fair and respectful way, and
not come down on them in a severe and hard manner,
condemning them for their mistakes because they were
unaware of the problems in life that all men face. (The
rich men of this present world have no idea how hard
the poor man struggles just trying to feed his family and
survive).

Therefore, Jesus, being a man, had to struggle through
life just as we struggle, and he personally knows the difficulties of trying to live and not sin. He was tempted in all
points as we are tempted, but he never sinned (Hebrews
4:15). The Hebrew author continued, "Wherefore it behooved him in all things to be made like unto his brethren, that he might become a merciful and faithful high
priest in things pertaining to God, to make propitiation
for the sins of the people. For in that he himself hath

suffered being tempted, he is able to succor them that are tempted" (Hebrews 2:17-18).

Because of the great love Jesus has for his children he died on a cross for them to take away their sins and give them eternal life. Therefore, because of that boundless love, he has great patience with them when they sin, and they are not quick to repent and return to him. Paul wrote, "Or despisest thou the riches of his goodness and forbearance and longsuffering, not knowing that the goodness of God leadeth thee to repentance?" (Romans 2:4).

When we read about men who sinned while living under the Old Covenant of Moses, and they were immediately punished for their transgression, such as Nadab and Abihu were punished; and we see men sin the same way today under the New Covenant of Christ, and they are not immediately punished, but seem to continue on with no consequences for their transgression whatsoever, we wonder—*Why?* The answer to that question is the cross, and the value of the great Sacrifice that was offered to God from the cross to take away the sins of the world, and put all sin away forever; that Sacrifice was the blood of God's only begotten Son. Therefore, it is because of that sacrifice, and the infinite value of that sacrifice, that God has great patience with men today, and it is God's tolerance and grace that gives men time to think and repent (Romans 2:4). John wrote, "For the law was given through Moses; grace and truth came through Jesus Christ" (John 1:17).

The law that was given through Moses, or any other law system offers absolutely no grace, it must be kept or the one who breaks it must pay the price for their disobedience. That is why the Old Testament Levitical law was so strictly enforced: it was law, it was severe, and it offered no grace except God allowing the sinner to offer an animal sacrifice to die in his place. Grace did not come until Jesus came, and he brought grace and truth into the world by his cross (John 1:17). Christians are not under law, they live by grace through faith, truth, and love (Romans 6:14-15), and the grace they live by is the grace Jesus brought with him into the world to give to all men by the way of his cross. Paul wrote, "For sin shall not have dominion over you: for ye are not under law, but under grace" (Romans 6:14). Thanks be to God that grace and truth came through Jesus Christ, and therefore the Almighty has great patience with men who sin, and it his grace and patience that gives them time to think and repent.

There were times when men were quite inquisitive about Jesus and who he was and where he came from. One such incident occurred when Jesus was entering Jerusalem in a manner prophesied by the prophet Zechariah. Zechariah prophesied to Israel that their King would come to them riding on an ass, even on a colt the foal of an ass (Zechariah 9:9). When Jesus commanded his disciples to bring him that colt, and he mounted it and rode it into Jerusalem, he was claiming to be the King of Israel, the Messiah. His actions caused quite a commotion, and men were asking, *"Who is this?"* Many believed he truly was the Messiah, the Son of God, and others were reluctant and did not believe. That caused a problem. Matthew wrote,

Now this is come to pass, that it might be fulfilled which was spoken through the prophet, saying, Tell ye the daughter of Zion, Behold, thy King cometh unto thee, Meek, and riding upon an ass, And upon a colt the foal of an ass. And the disciples went, and did even as Jesus appointed them, and brought the ass, and the colt, and put on them their garments; and he sat thereon. And the most part of the multitude spread their garments in the way; and others cut branches from the trees, and spread them in the way. And the multitudes that went before him, and that followed, cried, saying, Hosanna to the son of David: Blessed is he that cometh in the name of the Lord; Hosanna in the highest. And when he was come into Jerusalem, all the city was stirred, saying, Who is this? And the multitudes said, This is the prophet, Jesus, from Nazareth of Galilee. (Matthew 21:4-11)

There was another occasion when Jesus had finished his work for the day and it was evening, and he wanted to cross the sea and go to the other side. He and his disciples got into a boat, and they, with several other boats, started across the sea. When they were some distance from the shore a terrible storm ensued, and it threatened to sink the boat. Jesus spoke to the storm and rebuked it, and he calmed the sea. When Jesus stopped the storm and calmed the sea by just speaking to it, it caused his disciples to ask, "Who then is this, that even the wind and the sea obey him?" (Mark 4:41). Mark wrote of that event.

> And on that day, when even was come, he saith unto them, Let us go over unto the other side. And leaving the multitude, they take him with them, even as he was, in the boat. And other boats were with him. And there ariseth a great storm of wind, and the waves beat into the boat, insomuch that the boat was now filling. And he himself was in the stern, asleep on the cushion: and they awake him, and say unto him, Teacher, carest thou not that we perish? And he awoke, and rebuked the wind, and said unto the sea, Peace, be still. And the wind ceased, and there was a great calm. And he said unto them, Why are ye fearful? have ye not yet faith? And they feared exceedingly, and said one to another, Who then is this, that even the wind and the sea obey him. (Mark 4:35-41)

The fishermen in the boat were frightened of the storm, for they had seen many of them and they knew how dangerous they were. Many boats had been sunk by those storms, and many men had perished. But when they heard Jesus speak to the storm and immediately calm the sea, they were even more frightened, they were terrified of a man who had such great power that he could accomplish such an impossible task as speaking to a storm and calming a sea. Who was that man? He was the great *"I AM,"* Jesus, the Almighty himself.

There was another time when several men had a dear friend, and their friend had a severe case of palsy. That man's friends put him on a gurney so they could take him to Jesus because they knew he could heal him. It was some effort to get him to Jesus because the house where Jesus was teaching was so crowded they had to take their friend up on the roof, open the roof, and let him down into the room for Jesus to heal him.

Instead of Jesus healing him he forgave him of his sins, and that caused a problem. The Pharisees and doctors of the law were about to stone Jesus for blasphemy; they failed to see the miracle Jesus had just worked proved he had the power and the right to forgive the man of his sins. Luke wrote of that event.

> And it came to pass on one of those days, that he was teaching; and there were Pharisees and doctors of the law sitting by, who were come out of every village of Galilee and Judaea and Jerusalem: and the power of the Lord was with him to heal. And behold, men bring on a bed a man that was palsied: and they sought to bring him in, and to lay him before him. And not finding by what way they might bring him in because of the multitude, they went up to the housetop, and let him down through the tiles with his

couch into the midst before Jesus. And
seeing their faith, he said, Man, thy sins
are forgiven thee. And the scribes and the
Pharisees began to reason, saying, Who
is this that speaketh blasphemies? Who
can forgive sins, but God alone? But Jesus
perceiving their reasonings, answered
and said unto them, Why reason ye in
your hearts? Which is easier, to say, Thy
sins are forgiven thee; or to say, Arise and
walk? But that ye may know that the Son
of man hath authority on earth to forgive
sins (he said unto him that was palsied),
I say unto thee, Arise, and take up thy
couch, and go unto thy house. And immediately he rose up before them, and took
up that whereon he lay, and departed to
his house, glorifying God. And amazement took hold on all, and they glorified God; and they were filled with fear,
saying, We have seen strange things today. (Luke 5:17-26)

It might be noted that the scripture says that Jesus,
seeing their faith: Jesus, seeing the faith of the man's
friends who had the palsy, not the faith of the man who
had the palsy, is what healed the sick man of his disease.

An intelligent man who thinks in reasonable ways
would consider that if Jesus could heal a man with palsy
by just telling him to take up his bed and carry it home,
he certainly had the power to forgive him of his sins.

Jesus made that point clear when he said: "Which is easier, to say, Thy sins are forgiven thee; or to say, Arise and walk?" Anyone could tell a man his sins were forgiven, and that happens in some churches today. But no man can tell a person severely stricken with palsy to take up his bed and walk, and make it happen. When Herod the governor heard about the things Jesus was doing, he wondered: "Who is this? John I beheaded: but who is this, about whom I hear such things? And he sought to see him" (Luke 9:7-9).

All the questions men had about Jesus, and who he was, is what caused Jesus to ask his disciples a question; he asked, "But who do you say I am?" Matthew wrote,

> Now when Jesus came into the parts of Caesarea Philippi, he asked his disciples, saying, Who do men say that the Son of man is? And they said, Some say John the Baptist; some, Elijah; and others, Jeremiah, or one of the prophets. He saith unto them, But who say ye that I am? And Simon Peter answered and said, Thou art the Christ, the Son of the living God. And Jesus answered and said unto him, Blessed art thou, Simon Bar-Jonah: for flesh and blood hath not revealed it unto thee, but my Father who is in heaven. (Mathew 16:13-17).

Peter's response was, *Thou art the Christ, the Son of the living God.* Peter's reply was correct; he knew Jesus to be the Messiah, the Son of the living God, the true and great *"I AM."* That is the response all men should have if they are not prejudice, and they consider seriously the forces that worked in Jesus. The authority Jesus had to perform such great miracles could not possibly have been achieved by any other means than the power of God working in him.

There were times when Jesus was questioned about things he taught that other men did not believe, and they thought Jesus to be in error. One day the Sadducees came to Jesus and asked him a question to challenge him to prove there was going to be a resurrection of the dead—the Sadducees did not believe in spiritual things, and they did not believe there was going to be a resurrection of the dead (Acts 23:7-8). They did not believe a resurrection was even possible. It takes great faith to attend a memorial service for someone we have known and loved, and see a box containing that person's ashes, and believe those ashes shall live again in a new spiritual body. But such is true. Paul wrote, "So also is the resurrection of the dead. It is sown in corruption; it is raised in incorruption: it is sown in dishonor; it is raised in glory: it is sown in weakness; it is raised in power: it is sown a natural body; it is raised a spiritual body. If there is a natural body, there is also a spiritual body" (1 Corinthians 15:42-44).

The Sadducees led into their question in a way they thought would deceive Jesus and cause him to contradict himself. Their question was: If a man had more than one wife, when they all died and were called into heaven, which wife would be his lawful wife in heaven, for he was married to all of them? Jesus' response was as follows. Matthew wrote,

On that day there came to him Sadducees, they that say that there is no resurrection: and they asked him, saying, Teacher, Moses said, If a man die, having no children, his brother shall marry his wife, and raise up seed unto his brother. Now there were with us seven brethren: and the first married and deceased, and having no seed left his wife unto his brother; in like manner the second also, and the third, unto the seventh. And after them all, the woman died. In the resurrection therefore whose wife shall she be of the seven? for they all had her. But Jesus answered and said unto them, Ye do err, not knowing the scriptures, nor the power of God. For in the resurrection they neither marry, nor are given in marriage, but are as angels in heaven. But as touching the resurrection of the dead, have ye not read that which was spoken unto you by God, saying, I am the God of Abraham, and the God of Isaac, and the God of Jacob? God is not the God of the dead, but of the living. And when the multitudes heard it, they were astonished at his teaching. (Matthew 22:23-33)

Jesus answered their question by telling them there were no marriage relationships in heaven, and when men die their marriage is dissolved. But he also answered their question about there being a resurrection, and that was their real question. He told them that God is not the God of the dead, but of the living, therefore there shall be a resurrection. For the great *"I AM"* to be the God of the living *there must be a resurrection*; for Abraham, Isaac, and Jacob had all died. But they were not dead, they were just sleeping, for It was by the resurrection they lived, and Jesus is the resurrection and the life of all men, and that includes all men who have lived and died from Adam to the end of time. Jesus said, "I am the resurrection, and the life: he that believeth on me, though he die, yet shall he live; and whosoever liveth and believeth on me shall never die. Believest thou this?" (John 11:25-26). What a difference it makes to believe in Jesus! The reason Jesus could teach that those who die shall live again, and a man who lives shall never die—*if they believe in Jesus*—is because the resurrection makes death a sleep, a sleep for a while, possibly a long, long while, but not forever.

Jesus had a dear friend; his name was Lazarus. Lazarus became quite ill, and his sisters, Mary and Martha sent for Jesus to heal him. Jesus waited two days for Lazarus to die so he could raise him from the dead to glorify God (John 11:1-6). When Jesus knew Lazarus had died, he told his disciples that Lazarus had fallen asleep, and he must go and awake him. Jesus was going to prove death was just a sleep by raising Lazarus from the tomb. John wrote,

> These things spake he: and after this he saith unto them, Our friend Lazarus is fallen asleep; but I go, that I may awake him out of sleep. The disciples therefore said

unto him, Lord, if he is fallen asleep, he will recover. Now Jesus had spoken of his death: but they thought that he spake of taking rest in sleep. Then Jesus therefore said unto them plainly, Lazarus is dead. And I am glad for your sakes that I was not there, to the intent ye may believe; nevertheless let us go unto him. Thomas therefore, who is called Didymus, said unto his fellow-disciples, Let us also go, that we may die with him. (John 11:11-16)

Thomas had somewhat of a bent attitude. It was Thomas, *Doubting Thomas*, who would not believe Jesus had been raised from the dead, even when his brethren apostles insisted they had seen him alive and well. When Thomas finds out that Jesus wants to return to a place they had left not long ago, a place that was very dangerous for them to be, and now Jesus wants to return right back to it, he throws up his hands and he says, alright, let us go back with him, so we can die with him!

It was the occasion of Jesus raising Lazarus from his tomb that opened the way for him to teach his disciples that he was the resurrection and the life, and of all the times Jesus taught he was the *"I AM,"* this is one of the most important of those times to the Christian Community, for their eternal lives depend on it. The resurrection is essential for the cross to accomplish what God intended it to do, and that is to save the creation and all men from sin and death; but if there is no resurrection, then there is no cross.

When Jesus arrived at the tomb Lazarus had been in it four days. Martha was there to meet Jesus, and one of the first things she said to him was, Lord, if you had been here my brother would not have died! That was a stinging statement for Jesus to hear, and it must have cut him to the quick. Jesus told her that Lazarus would rise again, and Jesus meant it was going to happen very soon. Martha said she knew he shall rise again in the resurrection at the last day. (It is interesting Martha knew there was going to be a resurrection, for very few people knew that and even fewer believed it.) *Doubting Thomas* had been taught by Jesus himself that the resurrection was a fact, but he did not believe it, even after his disciples had witnessed to him they had seen Jesus alive. The only way Martha could have understood there was going to be a last-day resurrection was by being taught that by Jesus himself, and she, being smarter than Thomas, believed every word Jesus said as truth.

Mary did not go with Martha to meet Jesus when he came to Lazarus' tomb, and many of her friends were with her and consoling her, but when they saw Mary rise up quickly to go meet Jesus, they followed her, assuming she was going to the tomb to weep there. When Mary saw Jesus she fell at his feet, and said the same thing Martha said, "Lord, if you had been here my brother would not have died!" When they all went to the tomb, even Jesus, being perfectly human, suffered the same trauma all his disciples suffered, as John wrote below.

When Jesus therefore saw her weeping, and the Jews also weeping who came

with her, he groaned in the spirit, and
was troubled, and said, Where have ye
laid him? They say unto him, Lord, come
and see. Jesus wept. The Jews therefore
said, Behold how he loved him! But some
of them said, Could not this man, who
opened the eyes of him that was blind,
have caused that this man also should
not die? Jesus therefore again groaning in
himself cometh to the tomb. Now it was a
cave, and a stone lay against it. Jesus saith,
Take ye away the stone. Martha, the sis-
ter of him that was dead, saith unto him,
Lord, by this time the body decayeth; for
he hath been dead four days. Jesus saith
unto her, Said I not unto thee, that, if thou
believedst, thou shouldest see the glory
of God? So they took away the stone. And
Jesus lifted up his eyes, and said, Father,
I thank thee that thou heardest me. And
I knew that thou hearest me always: but
because of the multitude that standeth
around I said it, that they may believe that
thou didst send me. And when he had
thus spoken, he cried with a loud voice,
Lazarus, come forth. He that was dead
came forth, bound hand and foot with
grave-clothes; and his face was bound
about with a napkin. Jesus saith unto
them, Loose him, and let him go. Many
therefore of the Jews, who came to Mary

and beheld that which he did, believed on
him. But some of them went away to the
Pharisees and told them the things which
Jesus had done. The chief priests therefore and the Pharisees gathered a council,
and said, What do we? for this man doeth
many signs. If we let him thus alone, all
men will believe on him: and the Romans
will come and take away both our place
and our nation. (John 11:33-48)

What the Jews—the Pharisees and lawyers—feared
most, that they would lose their place and their nation if
they believed in Jesus, is exactly what they lost because
they did not believe in him.

When the disciples went to Lazarus' tomb there was
a large stone that covered its entrance, and it must be
removed by Jesus' disciples for him to call Lazarus out
of his grave. When the stone was removed, and Lazarus
was given life, he was in his grave clothes which were
very tight and very secure. He had to have someone release him from them or he could never have escaped
from them by himself, nor could he have removed the
face covering.

When Jesus was resurrected by his Father, his grave
clothes were just lying there in the tomb as if Jesus were
still in them, but he wasn't. John wrote,

Now on the first day of the week cometh
Mary Magdalene early, while it was yet
dark, unto the tomb, and seeth the stone
taken away from the tomb. She runneth

> therefore, and cometh to Simon Peter, and to the other disciple whom Jesus loved, and saith unto them, They have taken away the Lord out of the tomb, and we know not where they have laid him. Peter therefore went forth, and the other disciple, and they went toward the tomb. And they ran both together: and the other disciple outran Peter, and came first to the tomb; and stooping and looking in, he seeth the linen cloths lying; yet entered he not in. Simon Peter therefore also cometh, following him, and entered into the tomb; and he beholdeth the linen cloths lying, and the napkin, that was upon his head, not lying with the linen cloths, but rolled up in a place by itself. (John 20:1-7)

When the women went to Jesus' tomb to anoint Jesus' body, they wondered who would roll the stone away from the tomb entrance, for it was very large (Mark 16:1-4). When they arrived at the tomb, they saw it had been rolled away from the tomb entrance. It was an angel who removed that stone; he rolled it away, turned it over, and he sat on it (Matthew 28:1-3), and he told the women that Jesus was not in the tomb, he said, "He is not here; for he is risen, even as he said. Come, see the place where the Lord lay" (Matthew 28:6). That stone was not removed so Jesus could escape from the tomb, it was removed so the disciples could see there was no body in the tomb, for Jesus had been resurrected as he promised he would be.

Jesus' face napkin was neatly rolled up and placed away from the other grave clothes all by itself. That could only have been accomplished by someone helping Jesus do that, or by Jesus doing it himself, and there was no other person there. Lazarus had to have help to be released from his grave clothes and his face napkin.

It was wise of Jesus to say, *"Lazarus, come forth!"* or possibly many others would have risen right up with Lazarus and walked right out of their tombs. How foolish can men be when they see such great signs as Jesus accomplished, even to raising the dead, and not believe in him as the Son of God.

Jesus proved by what happened at Lazarus' tomb that he truly was the resurrection and the life, for when he spoke, and the power of his Father raised Lazarus from his tomb, it verified Jesus was everything he claimed to be.

Without Jesus' resurrection no other resurrections are possible, and even Lazarus' resurrection depended on Jesus' resurrection, and his resurrection was still in the future.

It appears beyond reason that men could witness Jesus' miracles, even to raising a man who had been dead four days, and instead of turning to him and believing in him, they wanted to stop him, because he was making waves in their religious system. They went to the Pharisees and reported to them what Jesus was doing, that he was raising the dead and he must be stopped. But what kind of power would it take to accomplish such a feat as to prohibit a man from raising the dead?

Jesus proved there will be a resurrection by raising Lazarus from his tomb, and he also proved the resurrection to be a fact when he spoke of his Father being the God of the living, not the God of the dead, and that makes death nothing more than a sleep.

There was a young man called Stephen who in the very beginning of the church left Judaism and became a Christian. Stephen was one of the seven men who had been chosen to become a deacon in the Lord's church. He was a spiritual man; a man full of faith and the Holy Spirit (Acts 6:5). Stephan was a brother who knew and understood the scriptures, and when he was challenged to explain to the scribes and the elders of the synagogue why he left Judaism to become a Christian—a dangerous decision to make because it caused him to become the first martyr (Acts 6:8-7:60)—he told them he left the Law of Moses to become a servant of the *Righteous One*: the very One whom they had betrayed and murdered (Acts 7:52). That Righteous One was the Almighty, the *"I AM,"* and it was He who appeared to Moses in the burning bush and told him he was the God of Israel's fathers. Stephen continued by telling the Jews that he was the One who would become the Messiah, the Christ, the Son of God and the Savior of all men; and it was he whom they had slain by nailing him to the cross. Stephen, speaking of that occasion said,

> And when forty years were fulfilled,
> an angel appeared to him in the wilder-
> ness of Mount Sinai, in a flame of fire
> in a bush. And when Moses saw it, he

wondered at the sight: and as he drew
near to behold, there came a voice of the
Lord, I am the God of thy fathers, the God
of Abraham, and of Isaac, and of Jacob.
And Moses trembled, and durst not behold. And the Lord said unto him, Loose
the shoes from thy feet: for the place
whereon thou standest is holy ground.
(Acts 7:30-33)

For Stephens discourse he was stoned to death, but
he did not die, he just fell asleep. Luke wrote, "And they
stoned Stephen, calling upon the Lord, and saying, Lord
Jesus, receive my spirit. And he kneeled down, and cried
with a loud voice, Lord, lay not this sin to their charge.
And when he had said this, he fell asleep" (Acts 7:59-60).
Stephen was a great saint and a great man of exceptional
faith and love.

There was another occasion when a little girl who was
twelve years of age; she was the daughter of the ruler of
a synagogue, and she died, but she also *just fell asleep.*
When she was very ill her father went to Jesus and asked
him to come to his house and heal her. Jesus went with
him, but he arrived at his house too late, and she had
died. Jesus told her father not to fret, that she was not
dead but asleep. Mark wrote,

And there cometh one of the rulers of the
synagogue, Jairus by name; and seeing
him, he falleth at his feet, and beseecheth
him much, saying, My little daughter is at
the point of death: I pray thee, that thou

come and lay thy hands on her, that she may be made whole, and live. And he went with him; and a great multitude followed him, and they thronged him...While he yet spake, they come from the ruler of the synagogue's house saying, Thy daughter is dead: why troublest thou the Teacher any further? But Jesus, not heeding the word spoken, saith unto the ruler of the synagogue, Fear not, only believe. And he suffered no man to follow with him, save Peter, and James, and John the brother of James. And they come to the house of the ruler of the synagogue; and he beholdeth a tumult, and many weeping and wailing greatly. And when he was entered in, he saith unto them, Why make ye a tumult, and weep? the child is not dead, but sleepeth. And they laughed him to scorn. But he, having put them all forth, taketh the father of the child and her mother and them that were with him, and goeth in where the child was. And taking the child by the hand, he saith unto her, Talitha cumi; which is, being interpreted, Damsel, I say unto thee, Arise. And straightway the damsel rose up, and walked; for she was twelve years old. And they were amazed straightway with a great amazement. (Mark 5:22-42)

Paul wrote about Christians who had fulfilled their lifetimes and had died. He said,

> But we would not have you ignorant, brethren, concerning them that fall asleep; that ye sorrow not, even as the rest, who have no hope. For if we believe that Jesus died and rose again, even so them also that are fallen asleep in Jesus will God bring with him. For this we say unto you by the word of the Lord, that we that are alive, that are left unto the coming of the Lord, shall in no wise precede them that are fallen asleep. For the Lord himself shall descend from heaven, with a shout, with the voice of the archangel, and with the trump of God: and the dead in Christ shall rise first; then we that are alive, that are left, shall together with them be caught up in the clouds, to meet the Lord in the air: and so shall we ever be with the Lord. Wherefore comfort one another with these words. (1 Thessalonians 4:13-18)

Those words, in which death is not mentioned, is called a *sleep*, and they are so very comforting to all who fear death, for in Christ and his kingdom *death does not exist*. Paul did not say the saints who left this world to go home to be with God had died, he said they had *fallen asleep*. Death is just a sleep, a long sleep, but nevertheless a sleep, and that is true because of the awaking all the dead shall experience when Jesus comes again, and they are resurrected (Acts 24:14-15).

According to the words of Paul, as written above, when Christ comes again all the saints who had fallen asleep, and their spirts had gone back to God, shall come with Christ when he comes again. Just think about *that* exciting moment! All the angels shall also come with him, and their job will be to separate the saints from the sinners to prepare them for the judgment (Matthew 13:49; 25:31-33). The saints shall stand on the right side of the throne of God for the judgment where they are protected by Jesus and his cross, for that is the side where Jesus sits. Those who are not in Christ shall stand on the left side of the throne of judgment, without Christ.

The reason for the saints' returning to this world with Christ when he comes again is for them to reenter their bodies that had died and bring them back to life—and it does not matter where their bodies were or what had happened to them. It takes the same power to give renewed life to a person who has been dead for one hour as it takes to raise one who has been dead for many years, or had been cremated, or who had perished at sea or in a fire.

When John wrote his revelation letter, he spoke of a first resurrection and a second death, but the second resurrection and the first death were not mentioned. It is not difficult to understand what John wrote if one believes that Jesus is the resurrection and the life of all the faithful. John wrote, "Blessed and holy is he that hath part in the first resurrection: over these the second death hath no power" (Revelation 20:6). When Jesus said, "I

AM the resurrection and the life," he established himself as being the *first resurrection* of all believers. When
a person believes in Jesus and confesses him to be the
Son of God, and they are baptized, they are immediately
forgiven of all their sins, they receive the gift of the Holy
Spirit (Acts 2:38), and they become a partaker of the *first
resurrection.* That is the moment when Jesus becomes
that person's life.

The first resurrection occurs the moment a person is
baptized, their sins are forgiven, and they are raised from
death to new life in Christ. We all have the power to be
partakers of the first resurrection if we so chose—*for that
is our choice.* The second resurrection, not mentioned in
John's letter, is the general resurrection of all the dead
when every person who has lived, and died, from Adam
to the end of time shall once again be brought back to
life (Acts 24:14-15). That shall happen when Jesus
comes again at the end of this age. When a person is a
partaker of the first resurrection, the second resurrection becomes the most perfect, the most secure, the most
beautiful, and the happiest moment that that person shall
ever experience; it is that moment all the saved wait for
and anticipate, and it is that moment the entire creation
is waiting for and expecting. Paul wrote,

> For the earnest expectation of the cre-
> ation waiteth for the revealing of the sons
> of God. For the creation was subjected to
> vanity, not of its own will, but by reason
> of him who subjected it, in hope that the
> creation itself also shall be delivered from

the bondage of corruption into the liberty of the glory of the children of God. For we know that the whole creation groaneth and travaileth in pain together until now. And not only so, but ourselves also, who have the first-fruits of the Spirit, even we ourselves groan within ourselves, waiting for our adoption, to wit, the redemption of our body. For in hope were we saved: but hope that is seen is not hope: for who hopeth for that which he seeth? But if we hope for that which we see not, then do we with patience wait for it. (Romans 8:19-25)

Paul believed when a person was raised from the watery grave of baptism to new life in Christ, they had truly experienced a resurrection. Paul wrote,

And you did he make alive, when ye were dead through your trespasses and sins, wherein ye once walked according to the course of this world, according to the prince of the powers of the air, of the spirit that now worketh in the sons of disobedience; among whom we also all once lived in the lusts of our flesh, doing the desires of the flesh and of the mind, and were by nature children of wrath, even as the rest:--but God, being rich in mercy, for his great love wherewith he loved us, even when we were dead through our trespasses, made us alive together with Christ (by grace have ye been saved), and raised us up with him, and made us to sit with him in the heavenly places, in Christ Jesus: that in the ages to come he might show the exceeding riches of his grace in kindness toward us in Christ Jesus: for by grace have ye been saved through faith; and that not of yourselves, it is the gift of God; not of works, that no man should glory. (Ephesians 2:1-9)

Possibly we have all experienced a baptism, and we ourselves have been baptized. What we see happen at a baptism, in this physical world, maybe in the church building or at a river, or wherever there is water (Acts 8:35-37), is a person who believes in Jesus confessing their faith—and then they are immersed in water, the watery grave of baptism, for the forgiveness of their sins (Acts 22:16) and to receive the gift of the Holy Spirit (Acts 2:38-39). We see a person immersed in water and getting wet, and we accept by faith that person has just been saved from sin and death.

But what happens at a baptism in the spiritual world is beyond description, it is utterly amazing. If we could see into the spiritual world what happens when a person is baptized, we would see a dead person, or a dead spirit seeking help, and finding that help by believing in Jesus as the Son of God, confessing their sins and their faith in Christ to forgive them, and then we see that dead person's body and spirit being buried, or immersed into the watery grave of baptism. When that person is raised up out of that water, *they are no longer dead*; they have been *born again* into a new life in Christ, and they shall never die again, for they have conquered what John called the second death, or spiritual death, and what Job called the king of terrors, (Job 18:14); they have been raised up out of that water, born of the water and the Spirit (John 3:5), to live a new life in a new world; that world being the kingdom of God, or the church. John wrote of how necessary it is to be born again.

> Now there was a man of the Pharisees, named Nicodemus, a ruler of the Jews: the same came unto him by night, and said to him, Rabbi, we know that thou art a teacher come from God; for no one can do these signs that thou doest, except God be with him. Jesus answered and said unto him, Verily, verily, I say unto thee, Except one be born anew, he cannot see the kingdom of God. Nicodemus saith unto him, How can a man be born when he is old? can he enter a second time into his mother's womb, and be Jesus answered, Verily, verily, I say unto thee, Except one be born of water and the Spirit, he cannot enter into the kingdom of God. That which is born of the flesh is flesh; and that which is born of the Spirit is spirit. Marvel not that I said unto thee, Ye must be born anew. The wind bloweth where it will, and

thou hearest the voice thereof, but knowest not whence it cometh, and whither it goeth: so is every one that is born of the Spirit. Nicodemus answered and said unto him, How can these things be? (John 3:1-9)

The first death, not mentioned in John's revelation letter, is the death Adam brought into the world when he sinned. God told Adam the day he ate of the Tree of the Knowledge of Good and Evil he would surely die (Genesis 2:16–17). Eve ate of the tree first, and then Adam. Eve ate of the tree because Satan's temptation was so strong she felt she could not resist— "*Why not?*" But Adam knew full well what he was doing when he ate of it (1 Timothy 2:13-15). Through their disobedience they brought sin and death into God's perfect world (Romans 5:12). At that moment they both died spiritually; they were separated from God when they were forced out of the garden and away from his presence (Genesis 3:22-24), and their bodies also started to age and die. Physical death for them was just a matter of time. Adam lived 930 years (Genesis 5:5) and the Bible does not mention how long Eve lived. The only woman in the Bible whose age was recorded when she died was Sarah, Abraham's wife (Genesis 23:1-2), and she was 127 years of age.

Adam and Eve were allowed to continue living in their bodies and in this world for many years after they had sinned, as are all men who have sinned allowed to continue in life. That is a great gift made possible by the grace of God, and it was given to allow sinners time to think, to repent, and accept God's forgiveness (Romans 2:4).

The second death is spiritual death, and God established it as the punishment for sin. Physical death takes place when the spirit and the soul are separated from the body—and the body dies (James 2:26). Spiritual death is separation from God, and that is the death all believers shall escape. Because of the resurrection there is no death for believers, but there are two deaths for unbelievers. There are two resurrections for believers, but only one resurrection for unbelievers, and the second resurrection shall occur when Christ comes again and all the dead are raised from their tombs to stand before Christ to be judged and sentenced (Acts 24:15; 2 Corinthians 5:10; Hebrews 9:27). The saints who stand on the right side of the throne of God shall hear their King say unto them, Come, ye blessed of my Father, inherit the kingdom prepared for you from the foundation of the world (Matthew 25:34). But the unbelievers who stand on the left side of the throne of God shall hear the king say unto them, Depart from me, ye cursed, into the eternal fire which is prepared for the devil and his angels (Matthew 25:41).

The death Adam caused was unconditionally decreed against all living creatures (Romans 5:12–21; 1 Corinthians 15:22; Hebrews 9:27). All living things die physically because of Adam's sin, and the proof of that fact is established in the death of little children. There are times when little children die, but they have never sinned (Matthew 18:1-6; Luke 18:15-17), therefore they die because Adam sinned, not because they had sinned.

But in every case it is the resurrection that annuls death and makes it a sleep.

The cross annulled the penalty for Adam's transgression the very moment Adam sinned, for by the grace of God Christ's sacrifice to take away the sins of the world was an established fact in God's mind before the foundation of the world (1 Peter 1:18-20). That is the reason no person was made a sinner or faced spiritual death because of Adam's transgression. Paul wrote, "For as in Adam all die, so also in Christ shall all be made alive" (1 Corinthians 15:22). "For as through the one man's disobedience the many were made sinners, even so through the obedience of the one shall the many be made righteous" (Romans 5:19). It took only one act of disobedience to make all men sinners, just as it took one act of obedience to make all men righteous. Thanks to Jesus the very same moment Adam's transgression made all men sinners was the same instant Jesus' obedience made all men righteous. He achieved that by annulling death and taking the judgment that was due to fall upon all men upon himself. Paul wrote, "...but hath now been manifested by the appearing of our Saviour Christ Jesus, who abolished death, and brought life and immortality to light through the gospel" (2 Timothy 1:10). Can one even begin to imagine the power it would take to *"abolish death?"* Therefore, we are all in perfect agreement when we believe that Adam's sin did not make anyone a sinner or pronounce the death sentence against anyone because of Adam's transgression, *but this author believes without the cross, that would not be the case.*

Adam's sin also condemned the entire creation and everything in it. Paul wrote,

> For the creation was subjected to vanity, not of its own will, but by reason of him who subjected it, in hope that the creation itself also shall be delivered from the bondage of corruption into the liberty of the glory of the children of God. For we know that the whole creation groaneth and travaileth in pain together until now. And not only so, but ourselves also, who have the first-fruits of the Spirit, even we ourselves groan within ourselves, waiting for our adoption, to wit, the redemption of our body. (Romans 8:20-23)

The cross is the power and the hope the creation has for complete deliverance from the condemnation it suffered because of Adam's transgression, and for the restoration of all things (Acts 3:19-21).

When a person is raised to new life in Christ by the first resurrection, Jesus immediately becomes that persons' life. Paul wrote,

> If then ye were raised together with Christ, seek the things that are above, where Christ is, seated on the right hand of God. Set your mind on the things that are above, not on the things that are upon the earth. For ye died, and your life is hid with Christ in God. When Christ, who is

our life, shall be manifested, then shall
ye also with him be manifested in glory. (Colossians 3:1-4)

When Christ becomes a person's life, they no longer have a life of their own, they have a much better
one; for they shall live *and reign* with Christ forever (2
Timothy 2:11-12) in a perfect spiritual kingdom. Paul
wrote, "Faithful is the saying: For if we died with him, we
shall also live with him: if we endure, we shall also reign
with him: if we shall deny him, he also will deny us" (2
Timothy 2:11-12).

For I through the law died unto the law,
that I might live unto God. I have been
crucified with Christ; and it is no longer I
that live, but Christ liveth in me: and that
life which I now live in the flesh I live in
faith, the faith which is in the Son of God,
who loved me, and gave himself up for
me. I do not make void the grace of God:
for if righteousness is through the law,
then Christ died for nought. (Galatians
2:19-21)

To be baptized into Christ and put on Christ (Galatians
3:27) is the most important decision a person can make
throughout their entire lifetime, for that decision determines where a person shall spend eternity. Jesus said, "He
that believeth and is baptized shall be saved; but he that
disbelieveth shall be condemned" (Mark 16:16). When
a person is baptized they are made one with Christ, and

they are given the life that Christ lives, which is perfect and forever. Paul wrote,

> What shall we say then? Shall we continue in sin, that grace may abound? God forbid. We who died to sin, how shall we any longer live therein? Or are ye ignorant that all we who were baptized into Christ Jesus were baptized into his death? We were buried therefore with him through baptism into death: that like as Christ was raised from the dead through the glory of the Father, so we also might walk in newness of life. For if we have become united with him in the likeness of his death, we shall be also in the likeness of his resurrection; knowing this, that our old man was crucified with him, that the body of sin might be done away, that so we should no longer be in bondage to sin; for he that hath died is justified from sin. But if we died with Christ, we believe that we shall also live with him; knowing that Christ being raised from the dead dieth no more; death no more hath dominion over him. For the death that he died, he died unto sin once: but the life that he liveth, he liveth unto God. Even so reckon ye also yourselves to be dead unto sin, but alive unto God in Christ Jesus. Let not sin therefore reign in your mortal body, that

ye should obey the lusts thereof: neither present your members unto sin as instruments of unrighteousness; but present yourselves unto God, as alive from the dead, and your members as instruments of righteousness unto God. For sin shall not have dominion over you: for ye are not under law, but under grace. (Romans 6:1-14)

When Christ went to the cross, his body died. That dead body was buried in a tomb. When we are baptized, we partake of his death by dying to self, to sin, and to this present world, and that *dead person* is buried in the watery grave of baptism just as Christ was laid to rest in his tomb. When Christ was raised from the tomb the third day, he lived again in a new world and with a new life. When a person is raised from the watery grave of baptism, they are in like manner raised with him to a new spiritual life in a new spiritual world. That says a lot for baptism.

When we are united with Christ to become one in him, we become partakers of his life and his glory forever. John wrote,

Behold what manner of love the Father hath bestowed upon us, that we should be called children of God; and such we are. For this cause the world knoweth us not, because it knew him not. Beloved, now are we children of God, and it is not yet made manifest what we shall be. We know

> that, if he shall be manifested, we shall be
> like him; for we shall see him even as he
> is. And every one that hath this hope set
> on him purifieth himself, even as he is
> pure. (1 John 1:1-3)

When Christ comes again and the dead are raised to new life by the general resurrection of all the dead, all the children of God, the living and those who had fallen asleep in Jesus, shall become just like Christ is now, and Christ was raised from the tomb to live in his glorious and perfect spiritual body (1 Corinthians 15:44) in a perfect and glorious spiritual world (2 Peter 3:13) forever. That is the time when the saints shall see Christ in all his glory as the Almighty himself, *even as he is*; and his children who view him shall be just like him—and that is the reason they shall be able to see him *even as he is*; it is because those who view him shall be spiritual beings just like him. The physical man cannot see into the spiritual world, but those in the spiritual world, who are spirits, can see into this physical world (John 8:56). Paul wrote, "but as it is written, Things which eye saw not, and ear heard not, and which entered not into the heart of man, whatsoever things God prepared for them that love him" (1 Corinthians 2:9). The spiritual world, or the kingdom of God However, we can know everything it is possible to know about the spiritual world if we believe in Jesus and abide in his Word (John 8:31-32).

When Jesus was raised from the dead, he lived in the same physical body he dwelt in before his death, and he lived in it for forty days (Acts 1:3). When Jesus ascended

into heaven his body changed from his physical body to
his spiritual body, for only a spiritual body can live in the
new spiritual world. Flesh and blood cannot inherit the
kingdom of God (1 Corinthians 15:50).

Jesus taught us that if we abide in his Word we shall
know the truth, and the truth shall make us free (John
8:31-32). He also taught us that he was the vine and we
are the branches, and when we abide in him we shall
bear much fruit. Both teachings are one and the same,
and both mean that when we abide in Christ we have life,
we know the truth, and we can accomplish many good
works for our Father. But we ourselves apart from Christ
have no life and can do nothing. Jesus said,

> I AM the true vine, and my Father is the
> husbandman. Every branch in me that
> beareth not fruit, he taketh it away: and
> every branch that beareth fruit, he cleans-
> eth it, that it may bear more fruit. Already
> ye are clean because of the word which I
> have spoken unto you. Abide in me, and I
> in you. As the branch cannot bear fruit of
> itself, except it abide in the vine; so nei-
> ther can ye, except ye abide in me. I AM
> the vine, ye are the branches: He that abi-
> deth in me, and I in him, the same beareth
> much fruit: for apart from me ye can do
> nothing. If a man abide not in me, he is
> cast forth as a branch, and is withered;
> and they gather them, and cast them into
> the fire, and they are burned. If ye abide in

me, and my words abide in you, ask whatsoever ye will, and it shall be done unto
you. Herein is my Father glorified, that ye
bear much fruit; and so shall ye be my disciples. Even as the Father hath loved me,
I also have loved you: abide ye in my love.
If ye keep my commandments, ye shall
abide in my love; even as I have kept my
Father's commandments, and abide in his
love.

These things have I spoken unto you, that
my joy may be in you, and that your joy
may be made full. This is my commandment, that ye love one another, even as
I have loved you. Greater love hath no
man than this, that a man lay down his
life for his friends. Ye are my friends, if
ye do the things which I command you.
No longer do I call you servants; for the
servant knoweth not what his lord doeth: but I have called you friends; for all
things that I heard from my Father, I have
made known unto you. Ye did not choose
me, but I chose you, and appointed you,
that ye should go and bear fruit, and that
your fruit should abide: that whatsoever
ye shall ask of the Father in my name, he
may give it you. (John 15:1-16)

Jesus' teachings were so powerful, so glorious, and so
awesome that many of the Jews thought they were just

too good to be true, and they thought Jesus' works were so amazing that they could not believe what they were seeing was real, and so Jesus was crucified for what he taught, what he did, and who he claimed to be.

Jesus pleaded with the Jews who were about kill him to believe the works he had achieved could only be accomplished by his Father working in him. Jesus said,

> If I do not the works of my Father, believe me not. But if I do them, though ye believe not me, believe the works: that ye may know and understand that the Father is in me, and I in the Father. They sought again to take him: and he went forth out of their hand. (John 10:37-39)

It is distressing that a man could do so much for his people, even to feeding their hungry, healing their sick, and raising their dead, and they would turn against him for the good works he had accomplished, and kill him. Jesus asked the Jews who were about to stone him, "Many good works have I showed you from the Father; for which of those works do ye stone me? The Jews answered him, For a good work we stone thee not, but for blasphemy; and because that thou, being a man, makest thyself God" (John 10:32-33).

There were some Jews who were intelligent enough to see what Jesus was doing could be accomplished by none other than the Almighty working in the one who achieved them. John wrote, "But of the multitude many believed on him; and they said, When the Christ shall come, will he do more signs than those which this man hath done?" (John 7:31).

One day when Jesus was in the temple, he had the opportunity to teach the Jews about who he was, where he came from, and what they could have if they believed in him. Jesus said, "I AM the light of the world, if you follow me ye shall not walk in darkness, but ye shall have the light of life" (John 8:12). Only a few Jews believed him, and Jesus said to them, "If ye abide in my word, then are ye truly my disciples; and ye shall know the truth, and the truth shall make you free" (John 8:31-32). When Jesus said that, even the Jews who believed him rebelled. John wrote,

> They answered unto him, We are Abraham's seed, and have never yet been in bondage to any man: how sayest thou, Ye shall be made free? Jesus answered them, Verily, verily, I say unto you, Every one that committeth sin is the bondservant of sin. And the bondservant abideth not in the house for ever: the son abideth for ever. If therefore the Son shall make you free, ye shall be free indeed. I know that ye are Abraham's seed: yet ye seek to kill me, because my word hath not free course in you. I speak the things which I have seen with my Father: and ye also do the things which ye heard from your father. (John 8:33-38)

Jesus was speaking to the Jews who believed him, but when he told them they must abide in His word to know the truth and to be made free, they immediately rebelled. Jesus could prove his doctrine was the truth, and he did so, not by his words, but by his works. When Jesus gave sight to a man who had been born blind (John, chapter 9), he proved he was the light of the world; and when he spoke to a friend who had been dead and in the tomb for four days, and said, "Lazarus, come forth" (John 11:43-44), and Lazarus came forth, Jesus proved he was the resurrection and the life. By Jesus' works he proved everything he taught was the absolute truth that could not be denied. Even so, their response was, We are Abraham's seed, we have never been in bondage to any man—we are free!

The Jews Jesus was teaching had forgotten their own history. They started out as a slave nation in bondage to Pharoah, and they had served the Egyptians for 430 years, and they were not free! (Exodus 12:40). They also had forgotten their seventy years bondage to Nebuchadnezzar in Babylon (Daniel 9:1-2). They did not remember the many, many times they were in bondage when they lived under the Judges because they refused to obey the Judges God gave them. In the letter to the Judges it is written,

> And the children of Israel again did that which was evil in the sight of Jehovah, and served the Baalim, and the Ashtaroth, and the gods of Syria, and the gods of Sidon, and the gods of Moab, and the gods of the

children of Ammon, and the gods of the Philistines; and they forsook Jehovah, and served him not. And the anger of Jehovah was kindled against Israel, and he sold them into the hand of the Philistines, and into the hand of the children of Ammon. And they vexed and oppressed the children of Israel that year: eighteen years oppressed they all the children of Israel that were beyond the Jordan in the land of the Amorites, which is in Gilead. And the children of Ammon passed over the Jordan to fight also against Judah, and against Benjamin, and against the house of Ephraim; so that Israel was sore distressed. And the children of Israel cried unto Jehovah, saying, We have sinned against thee, even because we have forsaken our God, and have served the Baalim. And Jehovah said unto the children of Israel, Did not I save you from the Egyptians, and from the Amorites, from the children of Ammon, and from the Philistines? The Sidonians also, and the Amalekites, and the Maonites, did oppress you; and ye cried unto me, and I saved you out of their hand. Yet ye have forsaken me, and served other gods: wherefore I will save you no more. Go and cry unto the gods which ye have chosen; let them save you in the time of your distress. And the children of

Israel said unto Jehovah, We have sinned:
do thou unto us whatsoever seemeth good
unto thee; only deliver us, we pray thee,
this day. (Judges 10:6-15)

Even the Jews who believed Jesus failed to understand the freedom Jesus was promising them was not
freedom from slavery, or freedom from being in bondage
to men, but freedom from sin, death, and even the law.
The last thing the Jews wanted was to be free from the
Law of Moses, for it was that law which was given only
to the Jews that made them God's chosen nation (Psalms
147:19-20). But Jesus wanted to free them from that law
because it was not a blessing, it was a curse. Paul wrote,

> For as many as are of the works of the law
> are under a curse: for it is written, Cursed
> is every one who continueth not in all
> things that are written in the book of the
> law, to do them. Now that no man is justi-
> fied by the law before God, is evident
> : for, The righteous shall live by faith;
> and the law is not of faith; but, He that
> doeth them shall live in them. Christ re-
> deemed us from the curse of the law, hav-
> ing become a curse for us; for it is writ-
> ten, Cursed is every one that hangeth on
> a tree: that upon the Gentiles might come
> the blessing of Abraham in Christ Jesus;
> that we might receive the promise of the
> Spirit through faith. (Galatians 3:10-14)

But now in Christ Jesus ye that once were far off are made nigh in the blood of Christ. For he is our peace, who made both one, and brake down the middle wall of partition, having abolished in his flesh the enmity, even the law of commandments contained in ordinances; that he might create in himself of the two one new man, so making peace; and might reconcile them both in one body unto God through the cross, having slain the enmity thereby: (Ephesians 2:13-16)

For it was the good pleasure of the Father that in him should all the fulness dwell; and through him to reconcile all things unto himself, having made peace through the blood of his cross; through him, I say, whether things upon the earth, or things in the heavens. And you, being in time past alienated and enemies in your mind in your evil works, yet now hath he reconciled in the body of his flesh through death, to present you holy and without blemish and unreproveable before him: if so be that ye continue in the faith, grounded and stedfast, and not moved away from the hope of the gospel which ye heard, which was preached in all creation under heaven; whereof I Paul was made a minister. (Colossians 1:18-23)

The Jews failed to understand the blessing of Abraham was not the Law of Moses and the priesthood of Levi, but it was Jesus coming to take away the sins of the world (John 1:29) by sacrificing himself to pay for all sin once for all, for all men, and do away with all law—except the law of Christ (Galatians 6:2), and the law of liberty (James 1:25; 2:12), which are the same law. The law of Christ is to live by faith (Habakkuk 2:4; Romans 1:17), and trust in God's grace (Ephesians 2:7-8) and his mercy (Titus 3:4-7).

The freedom Jesus offers to all men by knowing the truth and abiding in his Word is the greatest freedom anyone can experience. Paul wrote, "For freedom did Christ set us free: stand fast therefore, and be not entangled again in a yoke of bondage" (Galatians 5:1). Even a slave who worked on a plantation, or a bondservant who worked in the mines and suffered grievously, such as John suffered on the Isle of Patmos (Revelation 1:9), could have that freedom—when they believe in God and accept Jesus as their Savior. If a slave working on a plantation, or elsewhere, was a Christian, and the masters who owned him were not Christians, the slave had greater freedom than his masters.

What a great and wonderful blessing it is for all men of all nations to be offered the opportunity of becoming the family of God: the richest of the rich, the poorest of the poor, those who are free and those who are captive in prisons, are all promised this blessing; and the blessing is to be free from the fear of sin and death and have eternal life, and a perfect fellowship with God as his children forever—if only they will just believe in his Son and accept him as their Savior.

Jesus taught his disciples that he was the way out of death, and the Jews who heard him rebelled, and they asked him, Who do you think you are? Are you greater than our father Abraham, or the prophets who all died? Jesus' response was, I know who I AM. Jesus could not have made a clearer or more powerful statement declaring himself to be the resurrection and the life of all men than when he said, *"before Abraham was born, I AM."* Jesus affirmed it was he who was in the bush who commanded Moses to return to Egypt and deliver his children from bondage to Pharoah. That is when God Almighty declared himself to be the *"I AM,"* Jehovah, the covenant Name of the God of Israel, and he was known only to Moses and to the nation of Israel by that Name (Exodus 6:2-3), and that shall be his covenant name forever (Exodus 3:14-15). The Jews knew very well what Jesus was claiming, and they accused him of blasphemy. They picked up stones to stone him, and Jesus just left them and walked away. How he must have felt when he had given sight to the blind, healed the sick, and raised the dead, and they still refused to believe in him, and even wanted to kill him.

Death was established against all men because of sin. Ezekiel wrote,

> Behold, all souls are mine; as the soul of the father, so also the soul of the son is mine: the soul that sinneth, it shall die... The soul that sinneth, it shall die: the son

shall not bear the iniquity of the father,
neither shall the father bear the iniquity
of the son; the righteousness of the righteous shall be upon him, and the wick-
edness of the wicked shall be upon him.
(Ezekiel 18:4, 20)

Death is a very frightening experience that no one
shall escape. It is terrifying because it is certain, it is sud-
den, most people know very little about it, and it is forever. When we know that those who we love so dearly—
our wives, our husbands, our parents—are all going to
face death, there is no way we can prepare ourselves for
that event, it is something that can just tear our hearts
out. The only thing that softens that blow and gets us
through it is the name of Jesus. However, death can be
overcome and even turned into a victory—a victory because it is the only way out of this present evil world and
into the kingdom of God.

This author lives in Mexico, and in a Mexican *barrio*
(neighborhood), and next door to him lived a very old
man who had been a builder of houses, which means he
had laid many bricks and he had poured a lot of cement.
His name was Salvador. One day he told me he was getting very old and almost all his friends had died, and he
knew he was heading that way—and he did. He said they
all must have liked where they went when they died, because not one of them ever came back.

In Christ death can be overcome and even turned into
an escape, or a victory. Paul wrote,

Now this I say, brethren, that flesh and
blood cannot inherit the kingdom of
God; neither doth corruption inherit incorruption. Behold, I tell you a mystery:
We all shall not sleep, but we shall all be
changed, in a moment, in the twinkling of
an eye, at the last trump: for the trumpet
shall sound, and the dead shall be raised
incorruptible, and we shall be changed.
For this corruptible must put on incorruption, and this mortal must put on immortality. But when this corruptible shall
have put on incorruption, and this mortal
shall have put on immortality, then shall
come to pass the saying that is written,
Death is swallowed up in victory. O death,
where is thy victory? O death, where is
thy sting? The sting of death is sin; and
the power of sin is the law: but thanks be
to God, who giveth us the victory through
our Lord Jesus Christ. Wherefore, my beloved brethren, be ye stedfast, unmove-
able, always abounding in the work of the
Lord, forasmuch as ye know that your labor is not vain in the Lord. (1 Corinthians
15:50-58)

Christ overcame death and turned it into a victory
by suffering death himself. The only way Jesus had of
proving he had the power to overcome death was not

by living and never dying, but by dying and being raised from death by a resurrection.

When Jesus was crucified, he was declared dead by those who crucified him, and they knew when a man had died, or if he was still living. When Joseph of Arimathea, a councilor of honorable estate went to Pilate and asked him for Jesus' body, Pilate was amazed he had died so quickly. He asked the soldiers who crucified him if they were certain he was dead (Mark 15:43-45). They assured him Jesus was dead, and Pilate released his body for burial. Jesus was buried in a new grave where never a man had been laid (John 19:41), and there was a reason for that: When the disciples went to the tomb and they saw Jesus' body was not there, they did not have to count bodies to see if it was Jesus' body that was missing.

Jesus said, "When ye have lifted up the Son of man, then shall ye know that I AM, and I do nothing of myself, but as the Father taught me, I speak these things" (John 8:28). When Jesus was lifted up, crucified, buried, and raised from the tomb the third day, as Jesus predicted he would be, there was no doubt as to who he was: He truly was the Christ, the "*I AM*," the very one he claimed to be all the years of his ministry.

The Passover was one of the three religious festivals the Jews were commanded to keep, and it was one of the Passover feasts during Jesus' ministry that caused him to be terribly misunderstood. When the time came for the Passover to be celebrated Jesus went to Jerusalem to keep it. He entered the temple and stood amazed at the immorality and the greed that was taking place. Those in charge of the temple had turned it into a bazaar. They were selling the animals for the sacrifices at high profit, changing money, and making a grand business out of the temple and one of the Jews' most holy times. Jesus just sat down, made a scourge of cords, and with it He ran the animals out of the temple, poured out the money pots on the floor, and he told the Jews who were in charge of the temple that his Father's house was not a place of business. John wrote,

> And the passover of the Jews was at hand, and Jesus went up to Jerusalem. And he found in the temple those that sold oxen and sheep and doves, and the changers of money sitting: and he made a scourge of cords, and cast all out of the temple, both the sheep and the oxen; and he poured out the changers' money, and overthrew their tables; and to them that sold the doves he said, Take these things hence; make not my Father's house a house of merchandise. His disciples remembered that it was written, Zeal for thy house shall eat me up. The Jews therefore answered and said unto him, What sign showest thou unto us, seeing that thou doest these things? Jesus answered and said unto them, Destroy this temple, and in three days I will raise it up. The Jews therefore said, Forty and six years was this temple in building, and wilt thou raise it up in three days? But he spake of the temple of

his body. When therefore he was raised from the dead, his disciples remembered that he spake this; and they believed the scripture, and the word which Jesus had said. (John 2:13-22).

The Jews in charge of the temple services asked Jesus what gave him the right to cleanse the temple the way he had just purged it with such great force, and they wanted a sign proving he had the right to do that. That is when Jesus told them the sign he would give them: He said, "Destroy this temple, and in three days I will raise it up" (John 2:19). There is no way those Jews could understand the temple Jesus spoke of as being anything other than the temple he had just cleansed. But Jesus was not speaking of that temple; He was speaking of the temple of his body, that if they killed that temple, he would raise it up in three days—*Jesus was speaking of his resurrection.* That misunderstanding did not cause Jesus a problem until the end of his life when he had been arrested, and the Pharisees and elders were desperately looking for something they could charge him with so they could put him to death.

When Jesus was finishing his ministry and he was very close to the day of his crucifixion, he told his disciples he was going away to prepare a place for them (John 14:1-4). Jesus' crucifixion and his resurrection were the final works he had come into the world to accomplish. When he had finished them, he would enter his rest, just as his Father entered his rest when he had finished his work of creation; it was on the seventh day of the creation God entered into his rest (Genesis 2:1-3).

The disciples failed to understand where Jesus was going or what he was about to do. What Jesus wanted his disciples to understand was, there was a place for them with him and his Father, and it would be in a place—*a mansion*—where they would lack nothing and it would never end; it would be an eternal rest where they could live a perfect life forever where nothing would ever go wrong. It seems impossible to believe a place exists, but it does, and it exists because it is a kingdom that sin has never defiled.

Paul called the life the saints will have in their new home *life indeed*. Paul knew what kind of life the saints shall have in the next world because he had been there and experienced it (2 Corinthians 12:1-4). His earnest desire was to leave this world and return to the spiritual world he had enjoyed for such a short *"time"* (Philippians 1:21-24). That probably occurred when Paul was stoned in Lystra, and he died (Acts 14:19). Paul wrote,

> Charge them that are rich in this present world, that they be not highminded, nor have their hope set on the uncertainty of riches, but on God, who giveth us richly all things to enjoy; that they do good, that they be rich in good works, that they be ready to distribute, willing to communicate; laying up in store for themselves a good foundation against the time to come,

that they may lay hold on the life which is
life indeed. (1 Timothy 6:17-19)

Life indeed is real genuine life that is perfect; it is a life
that cannot get any better. Peter described that life when
he wrote,

> Blessed be the God and Father of our Lord
> Jesus Christ, who according to his great
> mercy begat us again unto a living hope by
> the resurrection of Jesus Christ from the
> dead, unto an inheritance incorruptible,
> and undefiled, and that fadeth not away,
> reserved in heaven for you, who by the
> power of God are guarded through faith
> unto a salvation ready to be revealed in
> the last time. (1 Peter 1:3-5)

The life the saints have in this present evil world, as
Paul called it (Galatians 1:4), is not perfect, it is not life
indeed, it is short, it ends in death, and there are many
disappointments, discouragements, hurts and blemishes
that just make the saints cry. All those imperfections
were caused by sin. That is not so in the world Jesus has
prepared for those who love him, because in that world
there is no sin and there is no death; and Jesus was about
to leave his disciples to go and prepare that place for
them.

Jesus called the life the saints will have in the world
to come *life abundantly*. Life abundantly means the saints
shall have super abundant life which is more life than
is necessary, for God's children overflow with life. Life

must be given to the one who has it by someone who *is* *life*, and that person is Jesus. John wrote, "In him was life; and the life was the light of men" (John 1:4). Paul wrote, "So also it is written, The first man Adam became a living soul. The last Adam became a life-giving spirit" (1 Corinthians 15:45).

Life is such a precious gift, and it is so valuable that *one day of life* cannot be purchased with all the wealth of the world; and yet most all the world takes it for granted that days and nights just happen, and they will continue on forever. The Psalmist wrote, "This is the day which Jehovah hath made; We will rejoice and be glad in it" (Psalms 118:24).

The time shall come when God will quit making days and this world will cease to exist. Therefore, we should thank God for every day we live and breathe, for it is a precious gift that can only be given by God. The older a person gets, the better he understands and accepts this. Death does not even exist in the world to come. John wrote,

> I am the door; by me if any man enter in, he shall be saved, and shall go in and go out, and shall find pasture. The thief cometh not, but that he may steal, and kill, and destroy: I came that they may have life, and may have it abundantly. I am the good shepherd: the good shepherd layeth down his life for the sheep. (John 10:9-11)

To have life indeed, and life abundantly, is more than a human mind can comprehend, because there is nothing like that in this world; therefore we just accept it by faith and press on enjoying all the good things God has given us while we look forward to the next life in the new world. It is our God *who is love* (1 John 4:8, 16) who has prepared that place for us, and he did so by the way of the cross of his only begotten Son.

John continued writing about the place where Jesus was going to prepare a place for his disciples.

> Let not your heart be troubled: believe in God, believe also in me. In my Father's house are many mansions; if it were not so, I would have told you; for I go to prepare a place for you. And if I go and prepare a place for you, I come again, and will receive you unto myself; that where I am, there ye may be also. And whither I go, ye know the way. Thomas saith unto him, Lord, we know not whither thou goest; how know we the way? Jesus saith unto him, I am the way, and the truth, and the life: no one cometh unto the Father, but by me. If ye had known me, ye would have known my Father also: from henceforth ye know him, and have seen him. Philip saith unto him, Lord, show us the Father, and it sufficeth us. Jesus saith unto him, Have I been so long time with you, and dost thou not know me, Philip? he that hath seen me hath seen the Father; how sayest thou, Show us the Father? Believest thou not

that I am in the Father, and the Father in
me? the words that I say unto you I speak
not from myself: but the Father abiding in
me doeth his works. Believe me that I am
in the Father, and the Father in me: or else
believe me for the very works' sake. (John
14:1-11)

Thomas asked Jesus a very reasonable question; he
asked, Lord, we do not know where you are going, how is
it possible for us to know the way? Thomas did not realize
he was looking at the Way. Jesus' response was, Thomas,
I AM the way, I AM the truth, and I AM the life, no one
comes to the Father but through me. No person shall
ever approach God, the Father, except through Jesus, his
Son, and the work Jesus accomplished to achieve that,
the resurrection being an essential part of his work.

That is what made Jesus the Door, for through him
is the only access anyone has to approach the Almighty
and enter his kingdom. Jesus said, "I AM the door; by
me if any man enter in, he shall be saved, and shall go in
and go out, and shall find pasture" (John 10:9). Once the
sheep leave the place where they had been kept and they
pass through *the door,* who is Jesus, they meet the Good
Shepherd, and Jesus is also that Good Shepherd. The
Good Shepherd loves his sheep so very much he would
lay down his life down to save them (John 10:11), and
that is exactly what Jesus did.

Ezekiel prophesied of the day when God's sheep, or
his children, would have the Good Shepherd to take care
of them, to provide for them, to protect them, and he

said that Good Shepherd would be *the Lord Jehovah God himself*. Ezekiel wrote,

> For thus saith the Lord Jehovah: Behold, I myself, even I, will search for my sheep, and will seek them out. As a shepherd seeketh out his flock in the day that he is among his sheep that are scattered abroad, so will I seek out my sheep; and I will deliver them out of all places whither they have been scattered in the cloudy and dark day. And I will bring them out from the peoples, and gather them from the countries, and will bring them into their own land; and I will feed them upon the mountains of Israel, by the watercourses, and in all the inhabited places of the country. I will feed them with good pasture; and upon the mountains of the height of Israel shall their fold be: there shall they lie down in a good fold; and on fat pasture shall they feed upon the mountains of Israel. I myself will be the shepherd of my sheep, and I will cause them to lie down, saith the Lord Jehovah. I will seek that which was lost, and will bring back that which was driven away, and will bind up that which was broken, and will strengthen that which was sick: but the fat and the strong I will destroy; I will feed them in justice. (Ezekiel 34:11-16)

When Jesus told his disciples he was the Good Shepherd, and he would search for his sheep who had gone astray, and he would lay down his life for his sheep, he was claiming to be Jehovah, the Good Shepherd Ezekiel spoke of, the great *"I AM."* John wrote,

> I am the good shepherd: the good shepherd layeth down his life for the sheep. He that is a hireling, and not a shepherd, whose own the sheep are not, beholdeth the wolf coming, and leaveth the sheep, and fleeth, and the wolf snatcheth them, and scattereth them: he fleeth because he is a hireling, and careth not for the sheep. I am the good shepherd; and I know mine own, and mine own know me, even as the Father knoweth me, and I know the Father; and I lay down my life for the sheep. And other sheep I have, which are not of this fold: them also I must bring, and they shall hear my voice: and they shall become one flock, one shepherd. (John 10:11-16)

Jesus is the Good Shepherd who's coming was prophesied by Ezekiel and being that good Shepherd he said he would lay down his life for his sheep. The Shepherd's responsibility to his sheep was to care for them, to protect them, to feed them, and to keep them safe at all costs, even when he must risk his own life to accomplish that.

David, the father of Jesus (Matthew 1:1), became a shepherd when he was very young. When his sheep were in danger from wild animals such as bears and lions, David risked his life by killing those enemies of his sheep. Samuel wrote of the time David left his sheep, as his father had commanded him, and he took food to his brothers who were in the Army—the Army of Israel that was fighting a war against the Philistines. The Philistines had a powerful army, and they had a giant warrior, some nine feet tall, who challenged the entire army of Israel. Samuel wrote,

> And there went out a champion out of the camp of the Philistines, named Goliath, of Gath, whose height was six cubits and a span.... And he stood and cried unto the armies of Israel, and said unto them, Why are ye come out to set your battle in array? am not I a Philistine, and ye servants to Saul? choose you a man for you, and let him come down to me. If he be able to fight with me, and kill me, then will we be your servants; but if I prevail against him, and kill him, then shall ye be our servants, and serve us. And the Philistine said, I defy the armies of Israel this day; give me a man, that we may fight together. And when Saul and all Israel heard those words of the Philistine, they were dismayed, and greatly afraid. (1 Samuel 17:4-11)

When David arrived at Israel's camp the war was on, he heard the words Goliath spoke, but David's brothers did not think he should even be there. Samuel wrote,

And David rose up early in the morning,
and left the sheep with a keeper, and took,
and went, as Jesse had commanded him;
and he came to the place of the wagons,
as the host which was going forth to the
fight shouted for the battle. And Israel
and the Philistines put the battle in array,
army against army. David left his baggage
in the hand of the keeper of the baggage,
and ran to the army, and came and saluted
his brethren. And as he talked with them,
behold, there came up the champion, the
Philistine of Gath, Goliath by name, out
of the ranks of the Philistines, and spake
according to the same words: and David
heard them. And all the men of Israel,
when they saw the man, fled from him,
and were sore afraid. And the men of
Israel said, Have ye seen this man that is
come up? surely to defy Israel is he come
up: and it shall be, that the man who killeth him, the king will enrich him with
great riches, and will give him his daughter, and make his father's house free in
Israel. And David spake to the men that
stood by him, saying, What shall be done
to the man that killeth this Philistine, and
taketh away the reproach from Israel? for
who is this uncircumcised Philistine, that
he should defy the armies of the living
God? And the people answered him after

this manner, saying, So shall it be done to
the man that killeth him.

And Eliab his eldest brother heard when
he spake unto the men; and Eliab's anger was kindled against David, and he
said, Why art thou come down? and with
whom hast thou left those few sheep in
the wilderness? I know thy pride, and
the naughtiness of thy heart; for thou
art come down that thou mightest see
the battle. And David said, What have I
now done? Is there not a cause? And he
turned away from him toward another,
and spake after the same manner: and the
people answered him again after the for-
mer manner.

And when the words were heard which
David spake, they rehearsed them before
Saul; and he sent for him. And David said
to Saul, Let no man's heart fail because of
him; thy servant will go and fight with this
Philistine. And Saul said to David, Thou
art not able to go against this Philistine to
fight with him; for thou art but a youth,
and he a man of war from his youth. And
David said unto Saul, Thy servant was
keeping his father's sheep; and when
there came a lion, or a bear, and took a
lamb out of the flock, I went out after him,
and smote him, and delivered it out of his

mouth; and when he arose against me, I caught him by his beard, and smote him, and slew him. Thy servant smote both the lion and the bear: and this uncircumcised Philistine shall be as one of them, seeing he hath defied the armies of the living God. And David said, Jehovah that delivered me out of the paw of the lion, and out of the paw of the bear, he will deliver me out of the hand of this Philistine. And Saul said unto David, Go, and Jehovah shall be with thee. (1 Samuel 17:20-33)

We know the rest of the story, and how David slew the giant (1 Samuel 17:48-50). All of that was accomplished because of David's great faith and the power of God working in him.

David was a good shepherd over his sheep, and he became the same good shepherd over the house of Israel, the shepherd of God's children. Christ is the Son of David, and he followed in David's footsteps, and he also became the Good Shepherd over the new house of Israel, *the Israel of God*, which is the church. Paul wrote, "For neither is circumcision anything, nor uncircumcision, but a new creature. And as many as shall walk by this rule, peace be upon them, and mercy, and upon the Israel of God" Galatians 6:14-16). "but if I tarry long, that thou mayest know how men ought to behave themselves in the house of God, which is the church of the living God, the pillar and ground of the truth" (1 Timothy 3:15).

Christ did not just protect his sheep at the risk of his life, he laid down his life as a Sacrifice to save his sheep from sin, death, and hades, and the Christians are his sheep. The pain and suffering Jesus suffered in giving his life to save his children is beyond understanding. The Hebrew author wrote of the high cost the Good Shepherd paid to make the saints' way to God possible. He wrote,

> Having therefore, brethren, boldness to enter into the holy place by the blood of Jesus, by the way which he dedicated for us, a new and living way, through the veil, that is to say, his flesh; and having a great priest over the house of God; let us draw near with a true heart in fulness of faith, having our hearts sprinkled from an evil conscience: and having our body washed with pure water. (Hebrews 10:19-22)

The good shepherd feeds his sheep in green pastures, and he makes sure they are led beside quiet waters where they can drink freely and safely (Psalms 23:1-2). So also, Jesus feeds his sheep, or his children, and he gives them water to drink—but the food and water Jesus provides for his children are spiritual food and water, for the soul, and not physical food and water for the body. Jesus said,

> Work not for the food which perisheth, but for the food which abideth unto eternal life, which the Son of man shall give unto you: for him the Father, even God, hath sealed. They said therefore unto him,

What must we do, that we may work the works of God? Jesus answered and said unto them, This is the work of God, that ye believe on him whom he hath sent. They said therefore unto him, What then doest thou for a sign, that we may see, and believe thee? what workest thou? Our fathers ate the manna in the wilderness; as it is written, He gave them bread out of heaven to eat. Jesus therefore said unto them, Verily, verily, I say unto you, It was not Moses that gave you the bread out of heaven; but my Father giveth you the true bread out of heaven. For the bread of God is that which cometh down out of heaven, and giveth life unto the world. They said therefore unto him, Lord, evermore give us this bread. Jesus said unto them, I am the bread of life: he that cometh to me shall not hunger, and he that believeth on me shall never thirst. (John 6:27-35)

Jesus had just performed a miracle in which he fed 5,000 men and their families with a few small fish and a piece of bread (John 6:1-15). Then he told his disciples to work for the spiritual bread which comes down out of heaven; bread that will give eternal life to all who eat of it, and it will satisfy their hunger and thirst forever. The disciples responded by requesting a sign, a miracle from Jesus to establish he was telling them the truth. How much more unreasonable could they be? He had just fed

5,000 men and their families with a few fish and a piece
of bread.

Spiritual hunger and thirst are just as real and intense
as are physical hunger and thirst. Spiritual hunger and
thirst is the strongest desire to know God and to have the
life he has promised, life that is perfect and forever. Jesus
is the only source of the bread and water that satisfies
spiritual hunger and thirst, and once Jesus satisfies them,
they are forever quenched.

Jesus' disciples cried out, Lord, give us this bread, for
they knew hunger and thirst only too well. Jesus told
them plainly; I AM the Bread of life that came down out
of heaven (John 6:34-35). To eat the bread Jesus offers
us, which is Jesus himself, is to believe him to be the Son
of God (John 8:24) and accept him as our God and our
Savior. It is to abide in his word and know the truth (John
8:31-32), and to be set free from sin and death by keeping his word (John 8:51).

Jesus, in like manner, is the water of life; and once
we drink of him we shall never thirst again, and we shall
have eternal life. We learn this by what Jesus taught the
Samaritan woman he met at a well, and Jesus made a special trip to Samaria just to meet that woman and teach
her (John 4:4). John wrote,

> There cometh a woman of Samaria to
> draw water: Jesus saith unto her, Give me
> to drink. For his disciples were gone away
> into the city to buy food. The Samaritan
> woman therefore saith unto him, How is
> it that thou, being a Jew, askest drink of

me, who am a Samaritan woman? (For Jews have no dealings with Samaritans.) Jesus answered and said unto her, If thou knewest the gift of God, and who it is that saith to thee, Give me to drink; thou wouldest have asked of him, and he would have given thee living water. The woman saith unto him, Sir, thou hast nothing to draw with, and the well is deep: whence then hast thou that living water? Art thou greater than our father Jacob, who gave us the well, and drank thereof himself, and his sons, and his cattle? Jesus answered and said unto her, Every one that drinketh of this water shall thirst again: but whosoever drinketh of the water that I shall give him shall never thirst; but the water that I shall give him shall become in him a well of water springing up unto eternal life. The woman saith unto him, Sir, give me this water, that I thirst not, neither come all the way hither to draw. (John 4:7-15)

Bread (or food) and water are two essential elements that are necessary for life to exist. A person can live about three days without water, and many more days without food. Once we have eaten the bread and have drunk the water they become part of us, and they keep us alive and give us strength and life. In the same manner, in the spiritual world, once we partake of Jesus, he becomes the food and the water that keeps our spirits and souls alive and gives us spiritual strength and spiritual life. Jesus said,

> I am the living bread which came down out of heaven: if any man eat of this bread, he shall live for ever: yea and the bread which I will give is my flesh, for the life of the world. The Jews therefore strove one with another, saying, How can this man give us his flesh to eat? Jesus therefore said unto them, Verily, verily, I say unto you, Except ye eat the flesh of the Son of man and drink his blood, ye have not life in yourselves. He that eateth my flesh and drinketh my blood hath eternal life: and I will raise him up at the last day. For my flesh is meat indeed, and my blood is drink indeed. He that eateth my flesh and drinketh my blood abideth in me, and I in him. As the living Father sent me, and I live because of the Father; so he that eateth me, he also shall live because of me. This is the bread which came down out of heaven: not as the fathers ate, and died; he that eateth this bread shall live for ever. (John 6:51-58)

The above scripture has nothing to do with the physical world, or with physical hunger and physical thirst, or with physical flesh and blood. It was Jesus' body, his flesh, that was nailed to the cross to take away the sins of the world, and it was his blood that washed away all sin.

Paul wrote, "And you, being in time past alienated and enemies in your mind in your evil works, yet now hath he reconciled in the body of his flesh through death, to present you holy and without blemish and unreproveable before him (Colossians 1:21-22). John wrote, "If we say that we have fellowship with him and walk in the darkness, we lie, and do not the truth: but if we walk in the light, as he is in the light, we have fellowship one with another, and the blood of Jesus his Son cleanseth us from all sin (1 John 1:6-7). To eat the flesh of Jesus and drink his blood is to spiritually accept Jesus as the Son of God and our Lord and Savior, and to accept his death on the cross as the real sacrifice that truly took away the sins of the world. Then, just as we put food and water into our bodies by eating and drinking them, we put Jesus into our spirits by accepting him in faith to be our Savior, our Master, and our new life (Galatians 2:20; Colossians 3:3-4). It was when Jesus was put to death in the flesh and made alive in the spirit that he became the spiritual food we must have to keep our spirits alive (1 Peter 3:18).

Jesus said to his disciples, "I AM the light of the world," and just as bread and water are essential elements for to life to exist on earth, so also are light and sight necessary. John wrote, "Again therefore Jesus spake unto them, saying, I am the light of the world: he that followeth me shall not walk in the darkness, but shall have the light of life" (John 8:12). Again, Jesus was teaching about a different kind of light than the light we experience from the sun, a light that illuminates physical objects on planet earth. Jesus was speaking of a spiritual light, the light that reveals God, and the life God that has given to all men who believe in him, and his Son—Jesus was speaking of the light that lights up life; a spiritual light that lights up spiritual life.

Jesus proved to his disciples he was the light of the world by healing a man who had been born blind. It was such a powerful miracle even those who witnessed it happening could not believe it really had (John, chapter 9).

Two of the several elements necessary for life to exist on planet earth are light and sight. Every living creature, from the smallest to the greatest, has eyes to see—and without eyes, life for them is not possible. All the works and all the accomplishments that have been achieved by men requires sight and light. A person who is blind must have someone to care for them, even to preparing their food, or they have extreme difficulty even surviving. When Jesus declared himself to be the light of the world, he proclaimed that without him life is not possible.

It is by Jesus' light that men can see God (Matthew 5:8), they can see where they came from, that they came from God, and his light opens the way for men to see how God wants them to live and function in this world—and what their reward will be for their faith and obedience (Hebrews 11:6).

When Jesus knew his ministry was coming to an end and he was close to the time he must die, he went to the garden of Gethsemane to pray. Jesus' disciples, and especially Judas knew of that place (John 18:1-2). Jesus went there for the express purpose of being arrested by the soldiers to face certain death by crucifixion. He knew his hour had come. He knew Judas had sold him out for thirty pieces of silver, and he knew he would be betrayed by the Judas' kiss. Matthew wrote, "Then one of the twelve, who was called Judas Iscariot, went unto the chief priests, and said, What are ye willing to give me, and I will deliver him unto you? And they weighed unto him thirty pieces of silver. And from that time he sought opportunity to deliver him unto them" (Mathew 26:14-16). When Judas came with the soldiers to arrest Jesus, Jesus knew exactly why they were there and what was going to happen. Matthew wrote,

> And while he yet spake, lo, Judas, one of the twelve, came, and with him a great multitude with swords and staves, from the chief priests and elders of the people. Now he that betrayed him gave them a sign, saying, Whomsoever I shall kiss, that is he: take him. And straightway he came to Jesus, and said, Hail, Rabbi; and kissed him. And Jesus said unto him, Friend, do that for which thou art come. Then they came and laid hands on Jesus, and took him. (Matthew 26:47-50)

Peter and the rest of the disciples did not know what Judas was doing, nor did they know Jesus was achieving exactly what he went to the garden to accomplish, and Peter drew his sword to protect Jesus. Matthew wrote,

> And behold, one of them that were with Jesus [Peter, John 18:10-11] stretched out his hand, and drew his sword, and smote the servant of the high priest, and struck

off his ear. Then saith Jesus unto him, Put up again thy sword into its place: for all they that take the sword shall perish with the sword. Or thinkest thou that I cannot beseech my Father, and he shall even now send me more than twelve legions of angels? How then should the scriptures be fulfilled, that thus it must be? (Mathew 26:51-54)

Jesus knew exactly why he was in that garden and exactly at that precise time; he went there to be betrayed by the Judas's kiss, more than most men could stomach, and then to be delivered up to Pilate to be crucified—and there was no way out, no escape.

Luke wrote, "While he yet spake, behold, a multitude, and he that was called Judas, one of the twelve, went before them; and he drew near unto Jesus to kiss him. But Jesus said unto him, Judas, betrayest thou the Son of man with a kiss?" (Luke 22:47-48). And when Peter struck Malchus, the high priest's servant with the sword and cut off his right ear, Jesus touched his ear, and healed him (Luke 22:51).

Jesus was so cooperative with the arresting force that came to the garden to capture him that they stood confused, and they wondered who this person could be who was in the garden where they had come to seize Jesus. So, Jesus had to help them arrest him. John wrote,

Judas then, having received the band of soldiers, and officers from the chief priests and the Pharisees, cometh thither

with lanterns and torches and weapons.
Jesus therefore, knowing all the things that
were coming upon him, went forth, and
saith unto them, Whom seek ye? They answered him, Jesus of Nazareth. Jesus saith
unto them, I am he. And Judas also, who
betrayed him, was standing with them.
When therefore he said unto them, I am
he, they went backward, and fell to the
ground. Again therefore he asked them,
Whom seek ye? And they said, Jesus of
Nazareth. Jesus answered, I told you that I
am he; if therefore ye seek me, let these go
their way: That the word might be fulfilled
which he spake, Of those whom thou hast
given me I lost not one. (John 18:3-9)

This would almost be comical if it were not so serious,
for when Jesus gave himself up so openly to be arrested
by the soldiers, it was something so unexpected they did
not know what to do, and they just fell all over themselves. After Jesus was arrested he was taken to the high
priest for questioning. The high priest forced Jesus to testify against himself, and that was contrary to the Law of
Moses, and the law of the Romans, and Jesus confronted
the high priest for committing such an error. John wrote,

The high priest therefore asked Jesus of
his disciples, and of his teaching. Jesus
answered him, I have spoken openly to
the world; I ever taught in synagogues,
and in the temple, where all the Jews

come together; and in secret spake I nothing. Why askest thou me? ask them that have heard me, what I spake unto them: behold, these know the things which I said. And when he had said this, one of the officers standing by struck Jesus with his hand, saying, Answerest thou the high priest so? Jesus answered him, If I have spoken evil, bear witness of the evil: but if well, why smitest thou me? Annas therefore sent him bound unto Caiaphas the high priest. (John 18:19-24)

Caiaphas could find no fault with Jesus, and so he asked him plainly if he were the Son of God, and he wanted a response that demanded death. Jesus gave him that response when he said, *"I AM."* Mark wrote of what happened next.

And they led Jesus away to the high priest: and there come together with him all the chief priests and the elders and the scribes. And Peter had followed him afar off, even within, into the court of the high priest; and he was sitting with the officers, and warming himself in the light of the fire. Now the chief priests and the whole council sought witness against Jesus to put him to death; and found it not. For many bare false witness against him, and their witness agreed not together. And there stood up certain, and bare false witness

against him, saying, We heard him say, I
will destroy this temple that is made with
hands, and in three days I will build another made without hands. And not even
so did their witness agree together. And
the high priest stood up in the midst, and
asked Jesus, saying, Answerest thou nothing? what is it which these witness against
thee? But he held his peace, and answered
nothing. Again the high priest asked him,
and saith unto him, Art thou the Christ,
the Son of the Blessed? And Jesus said, I
AM: and ye shall see the Son of man sitting at the right hand of Power, and coming with the clouds of heaven. And the
high priest rent his clothes, and saith,
What further need have we of witness-
es? Ye have heard the blasphemy: what
think ye? And they all condemned him to
be worthy of death. And some began to
spit on him, and to cover his face, and to
buffet him, and to say unto him, Prophesy:
and the officers received him with blows
of their hands. (Mark 14:53-65)

The Jews did not have the authority to execute anyone (Caesar had stripped them of that authority), and so
the high priest delivered Jesus up to Pilate to be judged
and executed, for Pilate had the power to do that—but
Pilate did not want anything to do with that case. The

Jews, according to their law, had already judged and condemned Jesus before he even had a trial. John wrote,

> They lead Jesus therefore from Caiaphas
> into the Praetorium: and it was early;
> and they themselves entered not into the
> Praetorium, that they might not be defiled,
> but might eat the passover. Pilate therefore
> went out unto them, and saith, What ac-
> cusation bring ye against this man? They
> answered and said unto him, If this man
> were not an evildoer, we should not have
> delivered him up unto thee. Pilate there-
> fore said unto them, Take him yourselves,
> and judge him according to your law. The
> Jews said unto him, It is not lawful for us
> to put any man to death: that the word of
> Jesus might be fulfilled, which he spake,
> signifying by what manner of death he
> should die. Pilate therefore entered again
> into the Praetorium, and called Jesus, and
> said unto him, Art thou the King of the
> Jews? Jesus answered, Sayest thou this
> of thyself, or did others tell it thee con-
> cerning me? Pilate answered, Am I a Jew?
> Thine own nation and the chief priests
> delivered thee unto me: what hast thou
> done? Jesus answered, My kingdom is not
> of this world: if my kingdom were of this
> world, then would my servants fight, that
> I should not be delivered to the Jews: but

now is my kingdom not from hence. Pilate
therefore said unto him, Art thou a king
then? Jesus answered, Thou sayest that I
am a king. To this end have I been born,
and to this end am I come into the world,
that I should bear witness unto the truth.
Every one that is of the truth heareth my
voice. Pilate saith unto him, What is truth?
And when he had said this, he went out
again unto the Jews, and saith unto them, I
find no crime in him. (John 18:28-38)

Pilate could judge a man only according to Roman law,
but he had nothing to do with Jewish law. The only ac-
cusation the Jews had against Jesus was that he was an
evil man. Pilate did not consider that a crime. The only
other charge the Jews could think of that might get Jesus
convicted was he claimed to be the King of Israel, and
therefore he was a threat to Caesar. Since the Jews had
no other charges against Jesus that would impress Pilate,
Pilate himself, contrary to Roman law, questioned Jesus
about what he had done and why he had been arrested
and brought before him. Pilate could not find any criminal charges against Jesus, and he wanted to release him
and let him go.

When Pilate understood Jesus had been brought before him for claiming to be the King of Israel, and the
Son of God, and he saw how Jesus responded to those
charges, with silence, Pilate was terrified! He went back
to Jesus and ask him, who are you and where are you

from? Jesus responded with silence. Pilate knew Jesus was no criminal, and so did Pilate's wife. Matthew wrote,

> Now at the feast the governor was wont to release unto the multitude one prisoner, whom they would. And they had then a notable prisoner, called Barabbas. When therefore they were gathered together, Pilate said unto them, Whom will ye that I release unto you? Barabbas, or Jesus who is called Christ? For he knew that for envy they had delivered him up. And while he was sitting on the judgment-seat, his wife sent unto him, saying, Have thou nothing to do with that righteous man; for I have suffered many things this day in a dream because of him. (Matthew 27:15-19)

The Jews would not accept Pilate just releasing Jesus, and so they demanded he be crucified. Pilate responded by abusing Jesus so badly by scourging and beating him, that he thought when the Jews saw him in such miserable condition they would be horrified and allow Pilate to release him, and they would just walk away. That did not happen. John wrote,

> Then Pilate therefore took Jesus, and scourged him. And the soldiers platted a crown of thorns, and put it on his head, and arrayed him in a purple garment; and they came unto him, and said, Hail, King of the Jews! and they struck him with

their hands. And Pilate went out again, and saith unto them, Behold, I bring him out to you, that ye may know that I find no crime in him. Jesus therefore came out, wearing the crown of thorns and the purple garment. And Pilate saith unto them, Behold, the man! When therefore the chief priests and the officers saw him, they cried out, saying, Crucify him, crucify him! Pilate saith unto them, Take him yourselves, and crucify him: for I find no crime in him. The Jews answered him, We have a law, and by that law he ought to die, because he made himself the Son of God. When Pilate therefore heard this saying, he was the more afraid; and he entered into the Praetorium again, and saith unto Jesus, Whence art thou? But Jesus gave him no answer. Pilate therefore saith unto him, Speakest thou not unto me? knowest thou not that I have power to release thee, and have power to crucify thee? Jesus answered him, Thou wouldest have no power against me, except it were given thee from above: therefore he that delivered me unto thee hath greater sin. Upon this Pilate sought to release him: but the Jews cried out, saying, If thou release this man, thou art not Caesar's friend: every one that maketh himself a king speaketh against Caesar. When Pilate therefore heard these words, he brought Jesus out, and sat down on the judgment-seat at a place called The Pavement, but in Hebrew, Gabbatha. Now it was the Preparation of the passover: it was about the sixth hour. And he saith unto the Jews, Behold, your King! They therefore cried out, Away with him, away with him, crucify him! Pilate saith unto them, Shall I crucify your King? The chief priests answered, We have no king but Caesar. Then therefore he delivered him unto them to be crucified. (John 19:1-16

When Pilate said, Shall I crucify your King? And the Pharisees, scribes, and elders responded by saying, We have no king but Caesar, it made clear how badly they hated Jesus. The entire Jewish population hated Rome, Caesar, Pilate, and everything about Rome, and they would never recognize that Rome had any authority over them whatsoever.

Pilate was quite severe with Jesus considering he did not think he was guilty of any crime. How could Pilate, a Roman ruler and judge treat a man so violently, and so shamefully, when he knew he was innocent of all wrongdoing?

Jesus declared himself to be the King of Israel and the Son of God, and he truly was (Matthew 27:11; John 18:37-38). Even Pilate the governor believed that if anyone was the king of the Jews, it was Jesus (John 19:19-22). Since Pilate had no other choice than responding to Jewish pressure, he delivered Jesus up to be crucified, but he wrote an inscription to place on Jesus' cross that conveyed to the Jews what he thought of Jesus. John wrote,

> And Pilate wrote a title also, and put it on the cross. And there was written, JESUS OF NAZARETH, THE KING OF THE JEWS. This title therefore read many of the Jews, for the place where Jesus was crucified was nigh to the city; and it was written in Hebrew, and in Latin, and in Greek. The chief priests of the Jews therefore said to Pilate, Write not, The King of the Jews; but that he said, I am King of the Jews. Pilate answered, What I have written I have written. (John 19:19-22).

It was those same accusations the leaders of Israel heaped upon Jesus when he was dying on the cross, and every one of the charges the Jews made against Jesus were absolutely true—he truly was the Son of God, and the king of Israel.

There were two robbers who were crucified with Jesus, and they had been with him for several hours while they were being accused and convicted of their crimes, and they were listening to all the charges that were being brought against Jesus. At first, when they were crucified with Jesus, they blasphemed him along with all the rest who were witnessing his crucifixion. Matthew wrote,

> Then are there crucified with him two robbers, one on the right hand and one on the left. And they that passed by railed o

n him, wagging their heads, and saying, Thou that destroyest the temple, and buildest it in three days, save thyself: if thou art the Son of God, come down from the cross. In like manner also the chief priests mocking him, with the scribes and elders, said, He saved others; himself he cannot save. He is the King of Israel; let him now come down from the cross, and we will believe on him. He trusteth on God; let him deliver him now, if he desireth him: for he said, I am the Son of God. And the robbers also that were crucified with him cast upon him the same reproach. (Matthew 27:38-44)

Everyone standing before the cross and witnessing the crucifixion, except for Jesus' disciples, were trying to make Jesus as miserable as possible as he was dying. Even the robbers who were dying with him joined in in their reproaches. Jesus had enough problems with the physical pain and agony he was enduring, but what he was about to suffer distressed him much more—the spiritual suffering he was about to endure! He was about to be made sin (2 Corinthians 5:21), and he was about to be forsaken of his Father to bear the punishment that all men deserved themselves for the sins they had committed, and Jesus was about to take all the sins of the world upon his own shoulders and pay for them in full with his life. That is when he cried out, "Eli, Eli, lama sabachthani? that is, My God, my God, why hast thou forsaken me?" (Matthew

27:46), and that is when Jesus became sin and took all the sins of the world upon himself, and he gave up his life, and he died.

One of the robbers, in just the few hours he had been with Jesus, came to the understanding of who Jesus was and why he had come. He must have been a very intelligent and observing man. He had noticed all the accusations, insults, injuries, and maltreatment that had been heaped upon Jesus and he himself had even joined in (Matthew 27:44). Then he observed how Jesus responded to such abuse—he just accepted it in silence, *and he said nothing.* Just before the three men died, with only minutes to live, one of the thieves had determined Jesus was being crucified for being exactly whom he claimed to be, the Son of God, the King of Israel, and the Savior of the world, and he believed all the accusations that were being heaped upon him were true—Jesus truly was the Son of God and the King of Israel. Luke wrote,

> And the people stood beholding. And the rulers also scoffed at him, saying, He saved others; let him save himself, if this is the Christ of God, his chosen. And the soldiers also mocked him, coming to him, offering him vinegar, and saying, If thou art the King of the Jews, save thyself. And there was also a superscription over him, THIS IS THE KING OF THE JEWS. And one of the malefactors that were hanged railed on him, saying, Art not thou the Christ? save thyself and us. But the other

answered, and rebuking him said, Dost thou not even fear God, seeing thou art in the same condemnation? And we indeed justly; for we receive the due reward of our deeds: but this man hath done nothing amiss. And he said, Jesus, remember me when thou comest in thy kingdom. And he said unto him, Verily I say unto thee, Today shalt thou be with me in Paradise. (Luke 23:35–43)

One of the robbers who were dying with Jesus looked to him and asked him to remember him when he came into his kingdom. Jesus said to him, *Today shalt thou be with me in Paradise.* This illustrates one of the greatest examples of faith, and one of the greatest acts of forgiveness of sin that can be found in the Bible. For here we see a dying man who was in great pain, and who confessed that he was dying a death he deserved for the terrible acts of violence he had committed (Luke 23:40–41) looking to another man who was dying with, him and asking that man to save him *after they had both died.* How did that man grasp all of that in just the few hours he had been with Jesus? That man had learned more about Jesus, who he was and why he came, than Peter and the rest of the apostles had learned in all the years they had been with him as his disciples (John 20:24-25). What an example this is to all believers, especially to those who at times feel they are not worthy to be saved and wonder if they really are because of how little they are able to accomplish for God, and because of how insignificant they truly are. Everyone who feels that way should remember this incident and know that they have as much to offer God as that thief had to offer in just the few moments before his life ended—all anyone has to offer God is their faith. That man was saved by his faith, and that is the only way anyone can be saved (Ephesians 2:8–9; 2 Timothy 1:9; Titus 3:3–7).

When the robber was saved and entered the kingdom of God (Luke 23:43), he became equal to all those who were in the kingdom of heaven, and that includes Noah, Abraham, Moses, David, Peter, Paul, and Mary; or any of the apostles. The reason for that being true is because no one who is in the kingdom of God is made great because of the magnitude of their own works or saved by their own accomplishments. We are all saved the same way, and that is by the grace of God through our faith (Ephesians 2:8–9; 2 Timothy 1:9; Titus 3:3–7). Everyone who enters the kingdom of heaven does so by the blood of Christ and what Christ has done for them, and not by what they have done for God. There is a parable in Matthew that verifies this, it is in Matthew 20:1–16. It is the parable of the laborers and the vineyard. Read it.

That does not mean there are no great saints in heaven; men and women who had lived an exceptional life of great faith and obedience, and whom God has recognized as special, and who has considered them to be extraordinary because of their outstanding faith and their great works. Even so, they are all still equal with each other as members of the family of God.

A father might have several children, some who have exceptional abilities and talents; maybe they are great musicians, they might be skilled in the academic world, or recognized for their great ability in the athletic world. Maybe that same father has a child, or other children who are quite normal, and maybe some with physical or mental problems. He might be very proud of his children who can accomplish great things, but he, as their father, loves all his children the same way, with the same passion and emotion, and he considers them all equal family members. A father does not love his children for what they can accomplish, he loves them because they are his children, and he is their father. That's just the way it is, and that is the way it is in the kingdom of heaven.

Here are some examples of God's children who were exceptional in their faith and works: Ezekiel wrote,

> And the word of Jehovah came unto me, saying, Son of man, when a land sinneth against me by committing a trespass, and I stretch out my hand upon it, and break the staff of the bread thereof, and send famine upon it, and cut off from it man and beast; though these three men, Noah, Daniel, and Job, were in it, they should deliver but their own souls by their righteousness, saith the Lord Jehovah. (Ezekiel 14:12-14)

Jeremiah wrote, "Then said Jehovah unto me, Though Moses and Samuel stood before me, yet my mind would not be toward this people: cast them out of my sight, and let them go forth" (Jeremiah 15:1).

When Jesus was on the Mount of Transfiguration with Peter, James, and John, there were two very special men who appeared to them in glory with Jesus; they were Elijah and Moses (Matthew 17:1-6). Moses was known as the great law-giver, and the care-taker of Israel as he led them through the wilderness to their promised land. Elijah was the great prophet of God who did not die, he was carried into heaven by a fiery chariot (2 Kings 2:11). Abraham was another man who was special to God because of his great faith, and even Paradise is called, *Abraham's Bosom* (Luke 16:22). James wrote,

> Was not Abraham our father justified by works, in that he offered up Isaac his son upon the altar? Thou seest that faith wrought with his works, and by works was faith made perfect; and the scripture was fulfilled which saith, And Abraham believed God, and it was reckoned unto him for righteousness; and he was called the friend of God. (James 2:21-23)

Abraham's reward for believing God and keeping God's word was outstanding. His faith rewarded him with being reckoned righteousness, and he was called a friend of God—and some of the promises of God that Abraham was required to believe and keep were very difficult, for they seemed impossible. In the case above, in James, it was the time Abraham was called to offer his son of promise on the altar of burnt offerings, and that meant Isaac, the son he had been promised and he had waited for, for twenty-five years, must die. Abraham never flinched, he just did it (Genesis 22:1-18).

When the writings of the Bible ended, and the Bible was completed, it did not stop men of exceptional faith and great works from existing. They do exist, and this author has known some such men whom he believes could stand right there with them.

What were the good works such men accomplished that made them so great? Were they great miraculous accomplishments—or something much simpler? When we understand what the greatest work a man can do for God is, and what the reward is for believing and achieving that work, we shall stand amazed.

The disciples asked Jesus that question; they asked, "What must we do, that we may work the works of God? Jesus answered and said unto them, This is the work of God, that ye believe on him whom he hath sent" (John 6:28-29). Such a simple thing, just believing God, and believing in his Son, that he truly is the Son of God, and to believe all he has told us to be the truth; and then living our lives to fulfill that truth is the greatest accomplishment any person can achieve for the Almighty—and when we make mistakes, and if we sin, we are forgiven. The Hebrew author wrote, "and without faith it is impossible to be well-pleasing unto him; for he that cometh to God must believe that he is, and that he is a rewarder of them that seek after him" (Hebrews 11:6). Abraham proved that to be the truth when he received his reward for just believing God's promises to be true, and then keeping them.

The last time the *"I AM"* appeared to anyone was when he appeared to Saul, a Pharisee, who was as devout a Jew as anyone could be. Saul was present when Stephan was stoned, and he agreed with the punishment Stephan received for leaving Moses to become a Christian. Luke wrote,

> And Saul was consenting unto his death. And there arose on that day a great persecution against the church which was in Jerusalem; and they were all scattered abroad throughout the regions of Judaea and Samaria, except the apostles. And devout men buried Stephen, and made great lamentation over him. But Saul laid waste the church, entering into every house, and dragging men and women committed them to prison. (Acts 8:1-3)

Saul was determined he was going to destroy the church and kill all the Christians. When God saw the zeal Saul had for Moses, he knew if such a man could be converted to Christ, he would have that same zeal for the church. But how could such a man be converted? It would take a powerful miracle to accomplish that, and it did. Saul was on a mission to Damascus to execute Christians when he met the Living God, the *"I AM."* Luke wrote, "But Saul, yet breathing threatening and slaughter against the disciples of the Lord, went unto the high priest, and asked of him letters to Damascus unto the synagogues, that if he found any that were of the Way, whether men or women, he might bring them bound to

Jerusalem" (Acts 9:1-2). It was on that missionary journey to Damascus when Saul met the Living God, the *"I
AM."* Luke wrote of that event in the letter of the Acts of
the apostle.

> And it came to pass, that, as I made my
> journey, and drew nigh unto Damascus,
> about noon, suddenly there shone from
> heaven a great light round about me. And
> I fell unto the ground, and heard a voice
> saying unto me, Saul, Saul, why persecut-
> est thou me? And I answered, Who art
> thou, Lord? And he said unto me, I AM
> Jesus of Nazareth, whom thou persecut-
> est. And they that were with me beheld
> indeed the light, but they heard not the
> voice of him that spake to me. And I said,
> What shall I do, Lord? And the Lord said
> unto me, Arise, and go into Damascus;
> and there it shall be told thee of all things
> which are appointed for thee to do. And
> when I could not see for the glory of that
> light, being led by the hand of them that
> were with me I came into Damascus.
>
> And one Ananias, a devout man accord-
> ing to the law, well reported of by all the
> Jews that dwelt there, came unto me, and
> standing by me said unto me, Brother Saul,
> receive thy sight. And in that very hour I
> looked up on him. And he said, The God of
> our fathers hath appointed thee to know

his will, and to see the Righteous One, and to hear a voice from his mouth. For thou shalt be a witness for him unto all men of what thou hast seen and heard. And now why tarriest thou? arise, and be baptized, and wash away thy sins, calling on his name.

And it came to pass, that, when I had returned to Jerusalem, and while I prayed in the temple, I fell into a trance, and saw him saying unto me, Make haste, and get thee quickly out of Jerusalem; because they will not receive of thee testimony concerning me. And I said, Lord, they themselves know that I imprisoned and beat in every synagogue them that believed on thee: and when the blood of Stephen thy witness was shed, I also was standing by, and consenting, and keeping the garments of them that slew him. And he said unto me, Depart: for I will send thee forth far hence unto the Gentiles. (Acts 22:6-21)

Paul went to the Gentiles, and his efforts were very successful. He established many churches throughout Asia and the world (Colossians 1:5-6), and he wrote letters to those churches which became a major part of the gospel. Of all the letters in the New Testament, Paul wrote thirteen of them. He did not write Hebrews, and we know that because he said he didn't write that letter (2 Thessalonians 3:16-18).

※

CHAPTER 4

"I AM" JESUS — HIGH PRIEST OF GOD FOREVER AFTER THE ORDER OF MELCHIZEDEK

AFTER JESUS WAS CRUCIFIED, buried, and resurrected, his Father appointed him to become a High Priest after the order of Melchizedek, just as Psalms 110:4 prophesied, and that qualified Jesus, as a man, to have the right
to become a priest and approach God directly—*as a man*.
Therefore, Jesus was the only Man who was authorized

to enter God's presence and present to his Father the sacrifice he had made on the cross. Summed up, Jesus was the only One ever who became a priest to offer himself as the perfect Sacrifice that would truly take away the sins of the world, and he was made a priest after the order of Melchizedek to accomplish that. The Hebrew author wrote,

> For every high priest, being taken from among men, is appointed for men in things pertaining to God, that he may offer both gifts and sacrifices for sins: who can bear gently with the ignorant and erring, for that he himself also is compassed with infirmity; and by reason thereof is bound, as for the people, so also for himself, to offer for sins. And no man taketh the honor unto himself, but when he is called of God, even as was Aaron. So Christ also glorified not himself to be made a high priest, but he that spake unto him, Thou art my Son, This day have I begotten thee: as he saith also in another place, Thou art a priest for ever After the order of Melchizedek. (Hebrews 5:1-6)

Until Hebrews chapter 7, Melchizedek had been a very mysterious person. He was mentioned only twice in the Old Testament; once when he met Abraham returning from the slaughter of the kings (Genesis 14:14-24), and again in Psalms 110:4 where it was prophesied that someone would become a high priest for ever after the order of Melchizedek. That *someone* was the Messiah, the Christ, and his name is Jesus. The Hebrew author wrote,

> For this Melchizedek, king of Salem, priest of God Most High, who met Abraham returning from the slaughter of the kings and blessed him, to whom also Abraham divided a tenth part of all (being first, by interpretation, King of righteousness, and then also King of Salem, which is, King of peace; without father, without mother, without genealogy, having neither beginning of days nor end of life, but made like unto the Son of God), abideth a priest continually. Now consider how great this man was, unto whom Abraham, the patriarch, gave a tenth out of the chief spoils. And they indeed of the sons of Levi that receive the priest's office have commandment to take tithes of the people according to the law, that is, of their brethren, though these have come out of the loins of Abraham: but he whose genealogy is not counted from them hath taken tithes of Abraham, and hath blessed him that hath the promises. But without any dispute the less is blessed of the better. And here men that die receive tithes; but there one, of whom it is witnessed that he liveth. And, so to say, through Abraham even Levi, who receiveth tithes, hath paid tithes; for

he was yet in the loins of his father, when
Melchizedek met him. (Hebrews 7:1-10)

The Hebrew author described Melchizedek as a man
who had no mother, he had no father, he had no birth
or beginning of his days, and he had no death or end of
life; he did not die! That makes it impossible to understand who he was, where he came from, or what happened to him. There are some who are of the opinion that
Melchizedek did have a mother, he did have a father, he
did have a beginning of his life, and he died; his days did
end. They explain their position against what the Bible
says by affirming there was no record of Melchizedek's
parents in the Bible, nor were his birth or his death recorded, and therefore it was just as if none of those things
existed, *but that is not what the Bible says.* Consider what
the Bible says, and what it says about Melchizedek, and
who that man was.

In Genesis 14:1–24, four very powerful kings had
attacked the five kings of Sodom, Gomorrah, and three
other villages. Abraham's nephew, Lot, lived in Sodom.
Those five kings had been paying taxes to the four kings
who attacked them for twelve years. The thirteenth year
they rebelled and quit paying, for they could pay no more
(Genesis 14:4–5). Abraham's nephew, Lot, and all his
family who lived in Sodom were taken captive with the
rest of the city, and all their possessions were stolen. The
possessions of the other four cities were taken as well.
When Abraham was told about that (Genesis 14:13–14),
Abraham took his 318 trained men and attacked the op-
pressors, the four kings, by night. He defeated them and

redeemed Lot and all the stolen goods. The two kings of Sodom and Gomorrah wanted to reward Abraham, but Abraham refused their offer. He did not want anyone thinking it was they who had made him rich. God was so very well pleased with what Abraham had accomplished that a very mysterious person appeared to him and blessed him. Maybe that person is the most unusual and mysterious person who is mentioned in the Bible. His name was Melchizedek. That person only appears here, in this moment of time, when he blessed Abraham, and Abraham paid tithes to him. It is possible that Melchizedek appeared at other times, such as in Genesis, chapter 18; and in Judges 6:11-27, but if so he was never called by the name Melchizedek. Moses described that rare meeting between Melchizedek and Abraham in the book of Genesis, where he wrote,

> And Melchizedek king of Salem brought forth bread and wine: and he was priest of God Most High. And he blessed him, and said, Blessed be Abram of God Most High, possessor of heaven and earth: and blessed be God Most High, who hath delivered thine enemies into thy hand. And he gave him a tenth of all. (Genesis 14:18–20)

There is only one other place in the Old Testament that mentions Melchizedek (Psalms 110:4), and that verse says the priesthood of Jesus shall be after the order of the priesthood of Melchizedek. If Jesus' priesthood was after the order of Melchizedek's priesthood, then their priesthoods must have been identical. If the priest-hood of Christ was inferior or superior in any way to the priesthood of Melchizedek, then Melchizedek's priest-hood could not have determined the order of Christ's priesthood. An inferior priesthood cannot determine the order of a superior priesthood, and that is the reason the priesthood of Christ was not ordered after the order of Aaron's priesthood. Aaron's priesthood could not repre-sent the priesthood of Jesus because their priesthoods were not identical. Both Aaron, as the priest of Israel, and his priesthood had many flaws, as will be discussed below—whereas both Melchizedek's priesthood and Jesus' priesthood had no flaws. Both Jesus as Priest, and Melchizedek as Priest, and their priesthoods, were per-fect, holy, and righteous in every respect. Jesus as Priest, after the order of Melchizedek as priest, also means that just as Jesus was perfect, holy, and righteous—so also was Melchizedek perfect, holy, and righteous—in fact, Melchizedek was the King of Righteousness and the King of peace (Hebrews 7:1–2). Please consider that state-ment seriously.

When Abraham met Melchizedek after his great vic-tory, it was Abraham who was blessed by Melchizedek, and it was Melchizedek to whom Abraham paid tithes. The Hebrew author wrote,

> For this Melchizedek, king of Salem, priest
> of God Most High, who met Abraham re-
> turning from the slaughter of the kings
> and blessed him, to whom also Abraham
> divided a tenth part of all (being first, by

> interpretation, King of righteousness, and then also King of Salem, which is, King of peace; without father, without mother, without genealogy, having neither beginning of days nor end of life, but made like unto the Son of God), abideth a priest continually. (Hebrews 7:1–3).

Both of those acts affirmed it was Melchizedek who was the greater man. But when Abraham lived on the earth, the father of the faithful, and the one to whom all the blessings of God had been promised, he was the greatest living man. Even heaven is called *Abraham's bosom* (Luke 16:22).

Therefore, Abraham was one of the greatest of all men who had ever lived. He was called the father of the faithful (Galatians 3:7–9). There were many great men and great women who were well pleasing to God, and Jesus said among all of them who were born of a woman there had not arisen a man greater than John the Baptist (Matthew 11:11). However, Abraham was just as great, but not greater. (Where did Jesus place himself when he made that statement? for Jesus was born of a woman. Jesus' statement must have meant there had never arisen a man greater than John the Baptist, but there had arisen many men who were just as great). But Melchizedek was greater because he was the Lord himself in human form, *and he was not born of a woman.* Melchizedek had no father, he had no mother, and he had no genealogy. He had no beginning of days or end of life, which means he was eternal. He was the Word in human form.

There have been many questions raised about Melchizedek's identity. Who was that man? How could he be the priest of the Most High God, and king, when no place on earth can be established as to where he was a priest, or over what city he ruled as the king? Melchizedek was the king of Salem, and Salem was not a place, Salem is peace; but it was not peace among men, it was peace with God. What people or nation did Melchizedek represent as their priest and king? Who, or what people appeared before God, but only through Melchizedek? If he was the priest of God Most High, then all men without exception, including Aaron, had only one access to God—that access was through Melchizedek. If that is not so then it causes a problem with Melchizedek being a priest who determined the order of Christ as Priest, and Melchizedek's priesthood determining the order of Jesus' priesthood. Jesus said that no man shall come to the Father but through him. John wrote, "Jesus saith unto him, I am the way, and the truth, and the life: no one cometh unto the Father, but by me" (John 14:6). Therefore, during the time of Melchizedek's priesthood no man could appear before the Father except through him.

For Melchizedek to be both priest and king he must have had a kingdom and a priesthood—but if so, where were they? Some have said he was king and priest in Jerusalem, but it does not say Jerusalem, it says Salem, and Salem means peace. It also means righteousness (Hebrews 7:1–2). It is possible Jerusalem did not exist at that time, only about five-hundred years after the flood, and if it did exist it was an insignificant little village. But

Salem means peace, and righteousness, and there was no place on earth called by either of those names.

Melchizedek can be none other than the Word or the Lord himself in human form because everything that was said about Melchizedek can also be said about Jesus, but it cannot be said about any other person. Melchizedek was *made like* the Son of God, and Jesus was both man and God; therefore, Melchizedek was also man and God. Melchizedek, and Jesus, were both kings and priests, and no other person in the entire Bible has ever filled both of those offices, priest and king, but Jesus and Melchizedek. Melchizedek was the king of righteousness and the king of peace. Jesus is the King of kings and Lord of lords (Revelation 17:14), and Jesus is also the King of righteousness, and the King, or Prince of peace, just as Jeremiah and Isaiah have written:

> Behold, the days come, saith Jehovah, that I will raise unto David a righteous Branch, and he shall reign as king and deal wisely, and shall execute justice and righteousness in the land. In his days Judah shall be saved, and Israel shall dwell safely; and this is his name whereby he shall be called: Jehovah our righteousness. (Jeremiah 23:5–6)

Jeremiah wrote that Jesus, the branch of David, shall reign as King and his name shall be called *Jehovah our righteousness*. Therefore, Jesus is the King of righteousness, and he has all power and all authority to execute justice and righteousness because he is their King. But so did Melchizedek. Paul wrote that Jesus was made to be the Christians' righteousness (1 Corinthians 1:30).

For a person to be the king of righteousness he must not only be holy and righteous himself, but he is the standard of righteousness, and he rules over righteousness. He is the one who determines who is righteous and who is not, and what is righteous and what is not. There is no man that has ever had such authority but Jesus and Melchizedek (Hebrews 7:1–3).

Melchizedek was the king of peace, which means he ruled over peace, and he was the standard of peace—but the peace that Melchizedek ruled over, and the peace that Jesus rules over is not peace among men, or peace among nations—*it is the peace between men and God.* Matthew wrote,

> Think not that I came to send peace on the earth: I came not to send peace, but a sword. For I came to set a man at variance against his father, and the daughter against her mother, and the daughter in law against her mother in law: and a man's foes shall be they of his own household. (Matthew 10:34-36)

John wrote about the peace we have with God because of Jesus and his coming, when he said, "Peace I leave with you; my peace I give unto you: not as the world giveth, give I unto you. Let not your heart be troubled, neither let it be fearful" (John 14:27). Paul wrote, "Being therefore justified by faith, we have peace with God through our Lord Jesus Christ; through whom also we have had our access by faith into this grace wherein we stand; and we rejoice in hope of the glory of God" (Romans 5:1–2).

Jesus is the King of Peace, or the Prince of peace, just as Isaiah has written.

> For unto us a child is born, unto us a son is given; and the government shall be upon his shoulder: and his name shall be called Wonderful, Counsellor, Mighty God, Everlasting Father, Prince of Peace. Of the increase of his government and of peace there shall be no end, upon the throne of David, and upon his kingdom, to establish it, and to uphold it with justice and with righteousness from henceforth even for ever. The zeal of Jehovah of hosts will perform this. (Isaiah 9:6-7)

When Paul wrote his letter to the Ephesians, he told his Ephesian brethren that Jesus is our peace. Paul wrote,

> But now in Christ Jesus ye that once were far off are made nigh in the blood of Christ. For he is our peace, who made both one, and brake down the middle wall of partition, having abolished in the flesh the enmity, even the law of commandments contained in ordinances; that he might create in himself of the two one new man, so making peace; and might reconcile them both in one body unto God through the cross, having slain the enmity thereby:

and he came and preached peace to you
that were far off, and peace to them that
were nigh: for through him we both have
our access in one Spirit unto the Father.
So then ye are no more strangers and so-
journers, but ye are fellow-citizens with
the saints, and of the household of God,
being built upon the foundation of the
apostles and prophets, Christ Jesus himself being the chief corner stone; in whom
each several building, fitly framed together, groweth into a holy temple in the Lord;
in whom ye also are builded together for a
habitation of God in the Spirit. (Ephesians
2:13–22)

The scripture written above makes it very clear that
Jesus is our peace with God, and not our peace with each
other or with the world.

Just as Melchizedek was the priest of God Most High,
so also is Jesus. He was chosen by God to fill that office
after the order of Melchizedek (Psalms 110:4). Hebrews
5:5–6 says, "So Christ also glorified not himself to be
made a high priest, but he that spake unto him, Thou art
my Son, This day have I begotten thee: as he saith also
in another place, Thou art a priest for ever After the order of Melchizedek." The point the Hebrew writer made
is—*just as God had declared Jesus to be his Son, he has also
affirmed that he has appointed him to be High Priest forever
after the order of Melchizedek.* Therefore, Melchizedek did

not appoint himself to be high priest, it was God who appointed him to that position.

There are other words that describe Melchizedek which also describe Jesus. Just as Melchizedek was without father, without mother, without genealogy, having neither beginning of days or end of life, so also was Jesus. Jesus was in the beginning with God as the Word (John 1:1–2), and He was the great *"I AM"* before Abraham was born (John 8:58). As God, Jesus is also without father and without mother, without genealogy, having neither beginning of days or end of life, for he is eternal. Therefore, it was Jesus, the Word, who was in a human body who appeared to Abraham as Melchizedek.

There are many questions about Melchizedek we cannot answer unless we view him as the Word of God in human form—questions such as: What and where were his kingdom and his priesthood? What people did he serve as priest of God Most High? How did they approach God through him? Before Christ, was there any person on this earth who could approach God without approaching him through Melchizedek, priest of the Most High God? If so, what was the purpose of his priesthood, and how could his priesthood determine the order of the priesthood of Christ (John 14:6)? Where did he come from to meet Abraham, and how did he know about Abraham's great victory over the five kings, and why did it matter to him? Where did Melchizedek go after he left Abraham? Melchizedek was not some obscure unimportant person who was sent by God to bless Abraham and to be the type of the priesthood of Christ, and then just vanish off the face of the earth. If Melchizedek was the exceedingly important king and priest as is stated in Genesis, and the Hebrew letter—a person even much greater than Abraham—and if his priesthood and kingdom were of this world, something would be known about him, his kingdom, his priesthood, and the people whom he served and represented to God as both their priest and their king. But there is nothing known about any of that. Also, there could be no such kingdom and priesthood on this earth such as Melchizedek's kingdom and priesthood, a kingdom of righteousness and peace in a world full of corruption and violence (Genesis 6:5–7)—that is, until Jesus established the church, and Jesus' church is not of this world. Maybe this is the answer to the question, "Who was Melchizedek and where did he come from? Where did he rule as priest and king?"

In the beginning God created a perfect world where sin did not exist (Genesis 1:31). In such a world the entire creation had a perfect relationship with God. There was no need for a go-between, a bridge, or a priest between man and God because God and his entire world had perfect fellowship with each other without one. But when Adam sinned, he died, and he was cut off from God. By his sin the entire human family died and was also cut off from the Almighty and stood condemned (Romans 5:12–21; 8:20–22). Adam's sin caused God to withdraw his presence from the holy world he had just created (Genesis 1:31) because Adam's sin made it quite unholy, for It had been completely contaminated by sin. Adam broke God's heart in the process and he pierced him through with many sorrows (Genesis 6:6). From that time on if a man wanted to approach God he must be invited by God to do so—but! —there would have to be someone between God and man to represent both parties in any such communications between them. That person would be called a priest, and he also would have to be just as holy and righteous as God himself is holy and righteous, or even he could not approach the Almighty, not even for himself. He would have to be like God as well as being a man—a man like all other men (Hebrews 5:1–4). That person would be called a priest, and a priest is a bridge between two points—those two points are man and God.

After Moses became God's man and his law had been established, Aaron, Moses' brother, was appointed by God to be the high priest for Israel. But Aaron represented only the nation of Israel, and not the Gentiles (Psalms 147:19–20). During the time between Adam and Moses, who was it that represented the people to God? Who represented the Gentiles to God from the time of Moses to the time of Christ? They did not have Moses' law, and they were not under any of his commandments, including keeping the Sabbath; and breaking the Sabbath was a capital crime for Israel. During those periods of time there were many people who wanted fellowship with God, men such as Enoch, the seventh from Adam (Genesis 5:21–24; Hebrews 11:5; Jude 1:14-15), Noah, Job, Abraham, and others—such as Cornelius in the New Testament (Acts, chapters 10 and 11). God shall not reject those men just because they had not been born into the nation of Israel, especially when it was before the nation of Israel existed, but they were born Gentiles.

The answer to that Question can only be Melchizedek. Otherwise, what would be the purpose of even mentioning him, and why would he be the priest of the Most High God if there were any other access to God other than through him? After Christ arrived, he became the only access to God, and no one could appear before God except through Him (John 14:6). But it was Melchizedek who determined the order of Christ's priesthood, and how his priesthood would function. Therefore, Melchizedek was the Word in human form, the same One who had created the heavens and the earth.

Jesus is the Word who became flesh (John 1:1–2, 14). After his death on the cross, and his resurrection, he was appointed by God to be the King and the Priest of the Most High God. Jesus had to have been a man to have been appointed to those grand positions (Hebrews 5:1–2). But so did Melchizedek have to be a man. God knew from the beginning that the Word would become flesh, a man. Therefore, even before Jesus died on the cross God considered him to be qualified to fill the office of High Priest. Just as God could forgive sin before Jesus had died on the cross to become a sin offering (2 Samuel 12:13), he could also establish a priesthood between men and God through him. In the mind of God, the cross, and all the blessings that resulted because of the cross, were established facts before he laid the foundation of the world (Ephesians 1:3–5; 1 Peter 1:17–20). Therefore, all the blessings of God that came by the way of the cross could be granted to all men from the time of Adam until the end of time. If this view is correct then Melchizedek's kingdom was the eternal kingdom of God—the kingdom of peace, and the kingdom of righteousness; and it was the Word (Melchizedek) who was the King and the Priest—the very position to which God appointed Jesus as the reward for his work of redemption after he had been raised from the dead (Matthew 28:16–20).

Melchizedek's kingdom and priesthood were between God and all men who lived between the time of Adam and the resurrection of Jesus, when, at that time, God appointed Jesus as King and High Priest after the order of Melchizedek, and not after the order of Aaron (Hebrews 7:11).

> Now if there was perfection through the Levitical priesthood (for under it hath the people received the law), what further need was there that another priest should arise after the order of Melchizedek, and not be reckoned after the order of Aaron? For the priesthood being changed, there is made of necessity a change also of the law. For he of whom these things are said belongeth to another tribe, from which no man hath given attendance at the altar. For it is evident that our Lord hath sprung out of Judah; as to which tribe Moses spake nothing concerning priests. And what we say is yet more abundantly evident, if after the likeness of Melchizedek there ariseth another priest, who hath been made, not after the law of a carnal commandment, but after the power of an endless life: for

it is witnessed of him, Thou art a priest
for ever After the order of Melchizedek.
For there is a disannulling of a foregoing
commandment because of its weakness
and unprofitableness (for the law made
nothing perfect), and a bringing in there-
upon of a better hope, through which we
draw nigh unto God. And inasmuch as it
is not without the taking of an oath (for
they indeed have been made priests without an oath; but he with an oath by him
that saith of him, The Lord sware and will
not repent himself, Thou art a priest for
ever); by so much also hath Jesus become
the surety of a better covenant. And they
indeed have been made priests many in
number, because that by death they are
hindered from continuing: but he, because he abideth for ever, hath his priesthood unchangeable. Wherefore also he
is able to save to the uttermost them that
draw near unto God through him, seeing
he ever liveth to make intercession for
them. For such a high priest became us,
holy, guileless, undefiled, separated from
sinners, and made higher than the heavens; who needeth not daily, like those
high priests, to offer up sacrifices, first
for his own sins, and then for the sins of
the people: for this he did once for all,
when he offered up himself. For the law

> appointeth men high priests, having infir-
> mity; but the word of the oath, which was
> after the law, appointeth a Son, perfected
> forever more. (Hebrews 7:11–28)

If Jesus' priesthood could not be reckoned after the order of the priesthood of Aaron because Aaron's priesthood was flawed, then his priesthood could not be reckoned after the order Melchizedek if his priesthood was also flawed. That means Melchizedek, his kingdom, and his priesthood had to be perfect, holy, righteous, and sinless, without beginning and without end, and it was only the Word who could fill that position.

Jesus could not be a priest after the order of Aaron, because Aaron died, and someone had to take his place. When the one who replaced him died it was necessary to replace him, and that became a reoccurring event. Jesus was the one and only person who ever filled his office as Priest (from Adam to this present time). There were none before him and there shall not be any after him as Priest of the Most High God. Also, because Aaron was a sinner, and Jesus was not, Aaron could not typify Jesus as priest, nor could his priesthood typify the priesthood of Christ (Hebrews 7:17–28). Doesn't that mean Melchizedek had to be a holy, righteous, and sinless man—a man who had no beginning, and a man who would have no end to represent Jesus in his priesthood? Such a man, other than the Word, has never existed.

This might present a question. When Aaron was the high priest for Israel, and he could approach God only one day a year on the Day of Atonement by entering the

Most Holy Place with the blood of an animal, first for his own sins, and then for the sins of the people (Hebrews 9:6–7), who was it Aaron appeared before in the Most Holy Place, or, who did he appear before to allow him to enter the Most Holy Place?—especially when he presented his own sacrifice to God first, for his own sins? Not even Aaron, as a sinner, could present his own sacrifice directly to God without going through a priest, and that priest was Melchizedek. If all of this is true it seems in this area things did not change much for Jesus after his resurrection. Before and after Jesus' resurrection he was King of Righteousness, King of Peace, Priest of God Most High, and there was no one who appeared before God, the Almighty, except through him (John 14:6).

John wrote, "Jesus saith unto him, I am the way, and the truth, and the life: no one cometh unto the Father, but by me" (John 14:6). When Jesus spoke those words he had not yet gone to the cross, he had not been raised from the dead to establish his priesthood, and he had not been appointed High Priest. Therefore, there has never been a time, except in the days before sin came into the world, when anyone could appear before the Almighty without going through a priest, or through Christ, the Word. Jesus is the only access to God that there has ever been from Adam, to Moses, to this present time. He said so, John 14:6. The Hebrew letter might shed a little light on this question.

> Now these things having been thus prepared, the priests go in continually into the first tabernacle, accomplishing the

services; but into the second the high priest alone, once in the year, not without blood, which he offereth for himself, and for the errors of the people: the Holy Spirit this signifying, that the way into the holy place hath not yet been made manifest, while the first tabernacle is yet standing; which is a figure for the time present; according to which are offered both gifts and sacrifices that cannot, as touching the conscience, make the worshipper perfect, being only (with meats and drinks and divers washings) carnal ordinances, imposed until a time of reformation. (Hebrews 9:6–10)

Before Christ and his resurrection, the way into the Holy Place was closed. Even when it was open on that one day a year, the Day of Atonement, the sacrifices that were taken into it did not offer perfection (Hebrews 10:1–4). But the sacrifice of Jesus on the cross and his priesthood do offer perfection. The Hebrew author wrote,

But Christ having come a high priest of the good things to come, through the greater and more perfect tabernacle, not made with hands, that is to say, not of this creation, nor yet through the blood of goats and calves, but through his own blood, entered in once for all into the holy place, having obtained eternal redemption. For if the blood of goats and bulls, and the ashes of a heifer sprinkling them that have been defiled, sanctify unto the cleanness of the flesh: how much more shall the blood of Christ, who through the eternal Spirit offered himself without blemish unto God, cleanse your conscience from dead works to serve the living God? (Hebrews 9:11–14).

The way into the true Holy Place where God lives was not made manifest until the day Jesus died on the cross. That was the day when the sin problem had been perfectly solved and corrected, the sins of the world had been taken away (John 1:29), and the veil between the holy place and the Most Holy Place was ripped in two from top to bottom—*declaring that it was God who ripped it open.* On that day the way into the Holy Place of God was opened for all men, for all time, but only through Jesus, God's Son. Matthew wrote,

And Jesus cried again with a loud voice, and yielded up his spirit. And behold, the veil of the temple was rent in two from the top to the bottom; and the earth did quake; and the rocks were rent; and the tombs were opened; and many bodies of the saints that had fallen asleep were raised; and coming forth out of the tombs after his resurrection they entered into the holy city and appeared unto many. Now the centurion, and they that were with him watching Jesus, when they

> saw the earthquake, and the things that
> were done, feared exceedingly, saying,
> Truly this was the Son of God. (Matthew
> 27:50–54)

The saints who came out of their graves when Jesus died, and after his resurrection they entered Jerusalem to be seen by many of their friends and brethren, must have been an event that was witnessed by many people. That event must also have been quite evident to the Roman soldiers who had witnessed the earth shaking, the darkness, and the saints coming out of their tombs—and it caused them to tremble, tremble, tremble—and to confess they had made a terrible mistake—they had crucified God's only begotten Son! (Matthew 27:54).

It was a horrible shame that after they took Jesus down from the cross, and things had somewhat stabilized and returned to normal, some priest went right back into that tabernacle and stitched that veil right back together, and once again separated themselves from God because they failed to see what God had done with the cross of his Son.

****

There are some who have a problem with God appearing as a man, in a human body, before Jesus was born to Mary as the Son of man. However, God can do whatever pleases him, and whatever he feels is necessary and right for him and his kingdom. There was an occasion when that did happen. It is recorded in Genesis 18. That Bible chapter describes a time when the Lord, Jehovah,

appeared to Abraham as a man. Moses wrote in Genesis
18:1–2,

> And Jehovah appeared unto him
> [Abraham] by the oaks of Mamre, as he
> sat in the tent door in the heat of the day;
> and he lifted up his eyes and looked, and,
> lo, three men stood over against him: and
> when he saw them, he ran to meet them
> from the tent door, and bowed himself to
> the earth.

Abraham's greeting was unusual unless Abraham had
recognized one of those men as someone whom he had
met before. Abraham had met two kings, Pharaoh, king of
Egypt (Genesis 12:10–20), and Abimelech, king of Gerar
(Genesis 20:1–5), but there is nothing mentioned about
Abraham bowing before either of those kings. Therefore,
one of the men Abraham saw before the oaks of Mamre
must have been Melchizedek, or the Word in human
form, for Abraham would probably not have bowed in
such a fashion before just another man. After Abraham
returned from the slaughter of the four kings, and he
met the kings of Sodom and Gomorrah, and Melchizedek
(Genesis 14:16–24), nothing is mentioned about him
bowing before any of them. Maybe, at that time Abraham
did not know who Melchizedek truly was.

One of the three men Abraham saw by the oaks of
Mamre was Jehovah. The other two were mighty angels,
possibly they were Michael and Gabriel, because one
of them started talking to Abraham about what he was
about to do, and he addressed himself as Jehovah. First,

he told Abraham that Sarah was going to have a child, and Sarah laughed (so did Abraham, Genesis 17:17). Moses wrote, "And Jehovah said unto Abraham, Wherefore did Sarah laugh, saying, Shall I of a surety bear a child, who am old? Is anything too hard for Jehovah? At the set time I will return unto thee, when the season cometh round, and Sarah shall have a son" (Genesis 18:13–14).

Jehovah began a discussion with Abraham about what he was going to do to Sodom and Gomorrah. Genesis 18:16–18 says, "And the men rose up from thence, and looked toward Sodom: and Abraham went with them to bring them on the way. And Jehovah said, Shall I hide from Abraham that which I do; seeing that Abraham shall surely become a great and mighty nation, and all the nations of the earth shall be blessed in him?"

But when the three men started toward Sodom and Gomorrah, only two of them left, and one of the men, Jehovah, stayed there with Abraham and continued the discussion with him. Genesis 19:1 says, "And the two angels came to Sodom at even; and Lot sat in the gate of Sodom: and Lot saw them, and rose up to meet them; and he bowed himself with his face to the earth." As far as we know, God did not appear to men as another man very often—but he did here, to Abraham, and he also appeared in human form to Abraham as Melchizedek.

Jehovah also appeared to Gideon as a man, he was one of Israel's judges. It is written in the book of Judges,

> And the angel of Jehovah came, and sat under the oak which was in Ophrah, that pertained unto Joash the Abiezrite: and

his son Gideon was beating out wheat in the winepress, to hide it from the Midianites. And the angel of Jehovah appeared unto him, and said unto him, Jehovah is with thee, thou mighty man of valor. And Gideon said unto him, Oh, my lord, if Jehovah is with us, why then is all this befallen us? and where are all his wondrous works which our fathers told us of, saying, Did not Jehovah bring us up from Egypt? but now Jehovah hath cast us off, and delivered us into the hand of Midian. And Jehovah looked upon him, and said, Go in this thy might, and save Israel from the hand of Midian: have not I sent thee? And he said unto him, Oh, Lord, wherewith shall I save Israel? behold, my family is the poorest in Manasseh, and I am the least in my father's house. And Jehovah said unto him, Surely I will be with thee, and thou shalt smite the Midianites as one man. And he said unto him, If now I have found favor in thy sight, then show me a sign that it is thou that talkest with me. Depart not hence, I pray thee, until I come unto thee, and bring forth my present, and lay it before thee. And he said, I will tarry until thou come again. And Gideon went in, and made ready a kid, and unleavened cakes of an ephah of meal: the flesh he put in a basket, and he put the broth in a pot, and brought it out unto him under the oak, and presented it. And the angel of God said unto him, Take the flesh and the unleavened cakes, and lay them upon this rock, and pour out the broth. And he did so. Then the angel of Jehovah put forth the end of the staff that was in his hand, and touched the flesh and the unleavened cakes; and there went up fire out of the rock, and consumed the flesh and the un-leavened cakes; and the angel of Jehovah departed out of his sight. And Gideon saw that he was the angel of Jehovah; and Gideon said, Alas, O Lord Jehovah! foras-much as I have seen the angel of Jehovah face to face. And Jehovah said unto him, Peace be unto thee; fear not: thou shalt not die. Then Gideon built an altar there unto Jehovah, and called it Jehovah-shalom: unto this day it is yet in Ophrah of the Abiezrites. (Judges 6:11–24)

He first addressed Gideon as the angel of Jehovah, but several times he also addressed him directly as Jehovah (Judges 6:14–16, 23–25). This should not be a problem for anyone. If God has personal business he wants to take care of himself, and if he cares enough about it not to send the very best, the mightiest angel, but to deal with the matter himself to make certain it is dealt with cor-rectly, he has all power and every right to do it that way.

It would be interesting to know if Jehovah ever appears as a man in this present world, and in this present time, to anyone, or for any cause, or for any reason. If so, it would be impossible for anyone to know such an event had occurred (Matthew 25:34–46). However, we do know that the angels are here continually in constant service to God and his saints as they persistently minister to God's people (Hebrews 1:13–14). Therefore, we should be very careful about our relationships with other people because some have entertained angels unaware. Hebrews 13:1–2 says, "Let love of the brethren continue. Forget not to show love unto strangers: for thereby some have entertained angels unawares." Not only is it possible to entertain angels unaware, it most certainly happens—the Bible says it happens, as they minister to us.

CONCLUSION

IN THIS PRESENT WORLD in which we all live, any person, anywhere, who desires to escape this present evil world and all its threatening ways—and even escape death—can do so by obeying the gospel and becoming a Christian to follow in the steps of Jesus (1 Corinthians 11:1; 2 Thessalonians 1:5-10; 1 Peter 4:17). It does not matter what a person's occupation is for them to become a noble saint in the kingdom of God, one does not have to be a preacher or a teacher, or an elder or a deacon in the church to be an impressive saint. If a person is a doctor, a lawyer, or an Indian chief; a butcher a baker or a mechanic, he can be a great saint by his faith. It is not our works that make us great in the kingdom of God, it is our faith in believing Jesus to be the Son of God and abiding in his Word that causes God to have great respect for us, and pleasure in us (John 6:28-29). It is the work God has done for us that makes a person a great saint.

A person who labors in this world to make a living for himself and his family, and they are a Christian, and they give of their means to support the work of the church, are just as important as a preacher or an elder who works full time for the church and is supported by the church. Without the support of the working person in the church, there is no funding to support preachers or any other expense that is necessary for the church to function. Therefore, a person who labors in the secular world for his living and gives to the church is just as much a full-time worker for the Lord as is the preacher.

There are fewer rich men in the kingdom of God than the common man or the poor man, maybe that is because there are fewer of them. Abraham Lincoln said, *God must love the common man because he has made so many of them.* But a rich man has his thoughts on this world and his wealth. A poor man is looking for something better, and a better way of life, and they find that way in the church. There certainly are exceptions in both cases.

The rich have little awareness of how difficult it is for a poor man to work every day just to try to make enough to feed himself and his family, because a person must be in that situation to understand how difficult and inconvenient it is. I read a story about a very wealthy man who lived in what was almost a castle, with many possessions. He had a friend, perhaps a servant, who was struggling just to survive, and he was a Christian. One day the rich man wanted to show his friend all his precious things, and it took him some time to do so. During that entire time the servant observed all the precious things he saw, he said nothing. The rich man was somewhat confused by the servant's silence. When the show came to an end the rich man said, well, what do you think about all of this, and all that you have seen? The servant's response was: It must be possessing all of these things that makes it so very difficult for you to die.

El Fin

www.ingramcontent.com/pod-product-compliance
Lightning Source LLC
LaVergne TN
LVHW011226080426
835509LV00005B/339

* 9 7 8 1 6 3 3 5 7 4 4 1 0 *